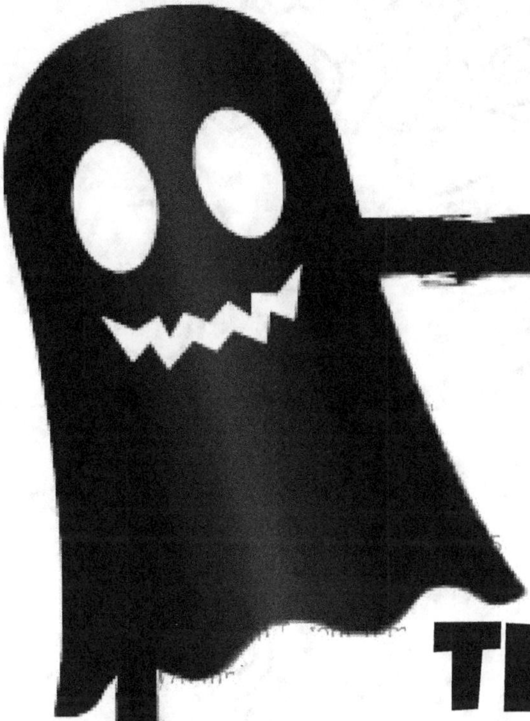

THIS BOOK BELONGS TO

Nano

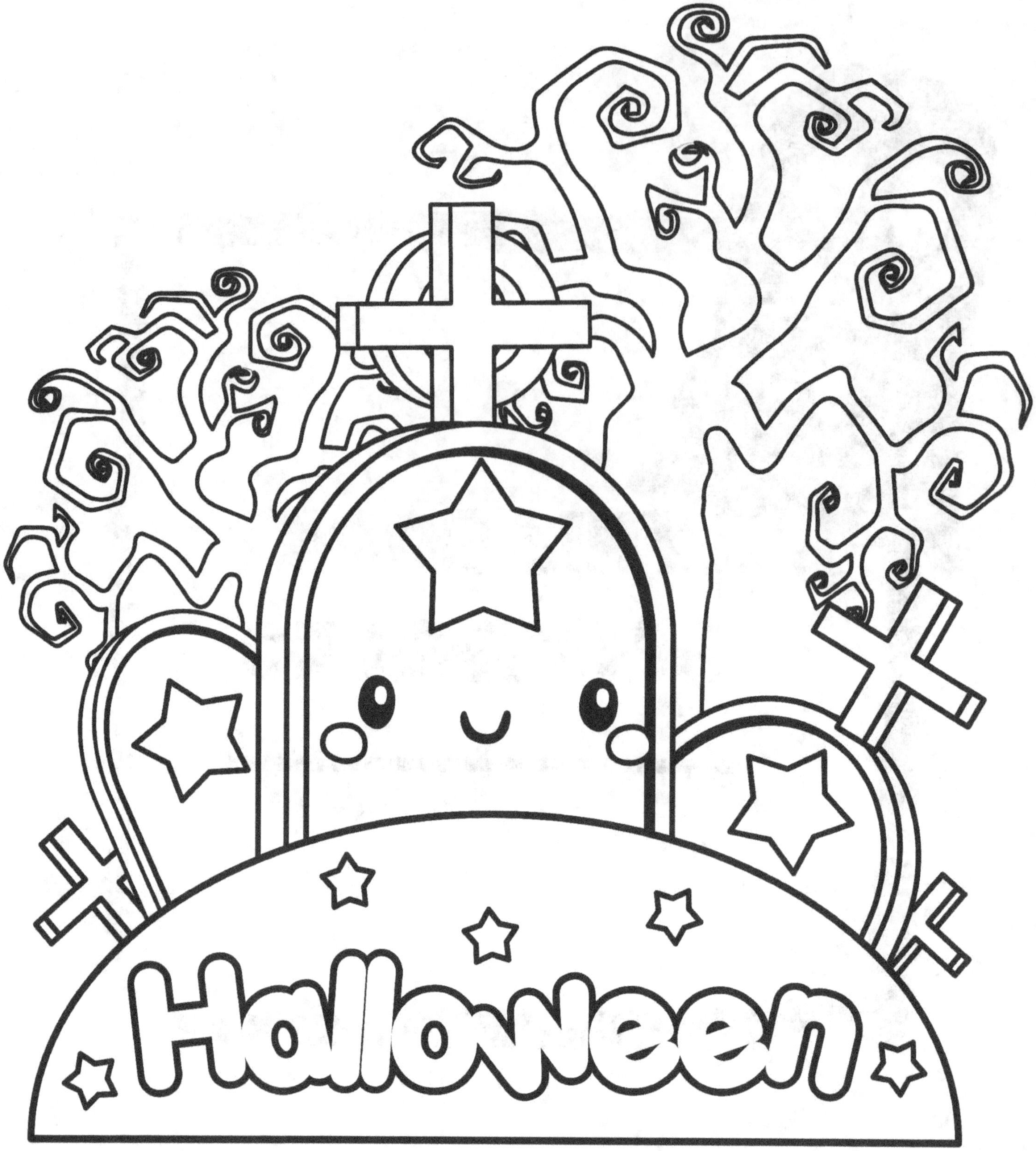
Halloween

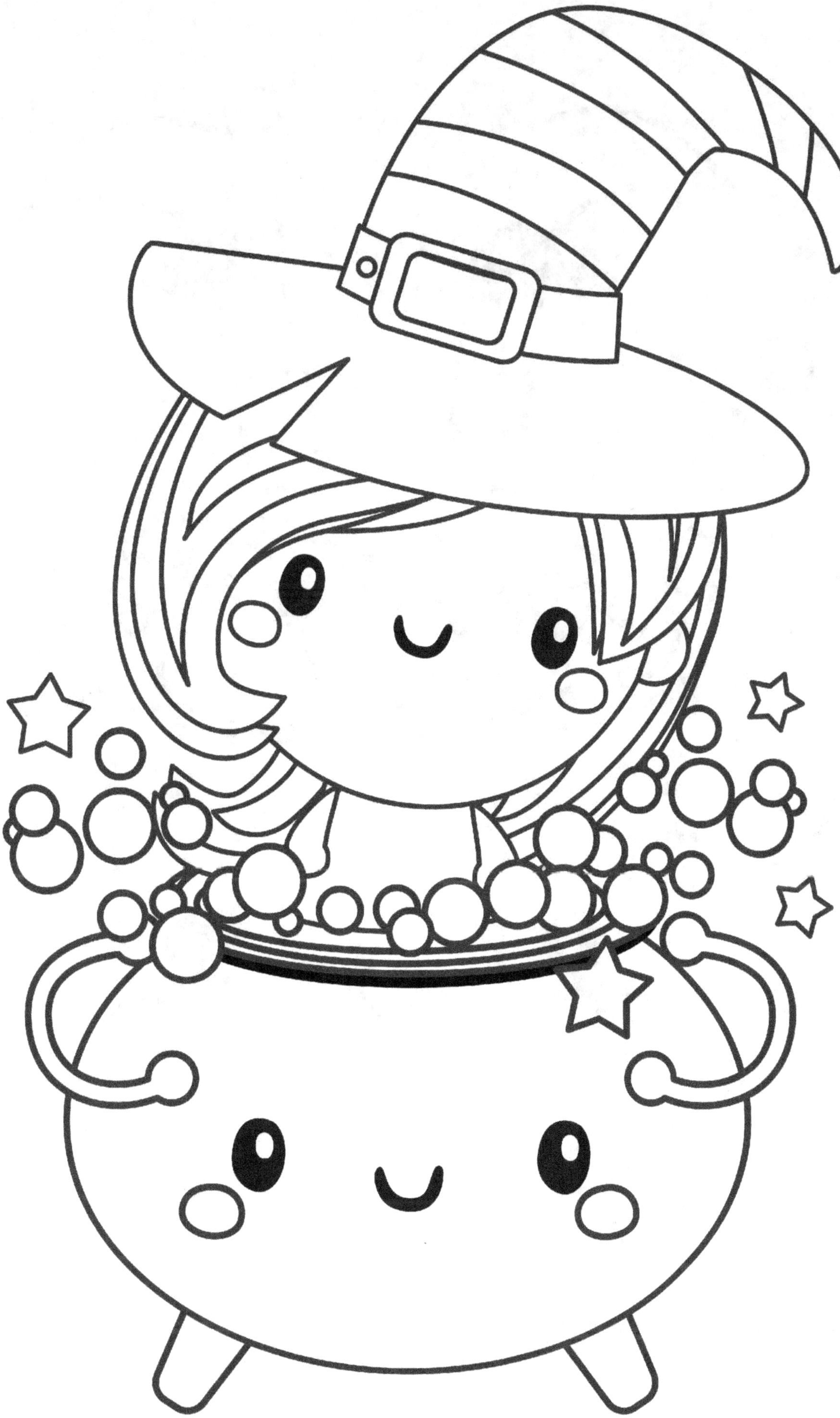

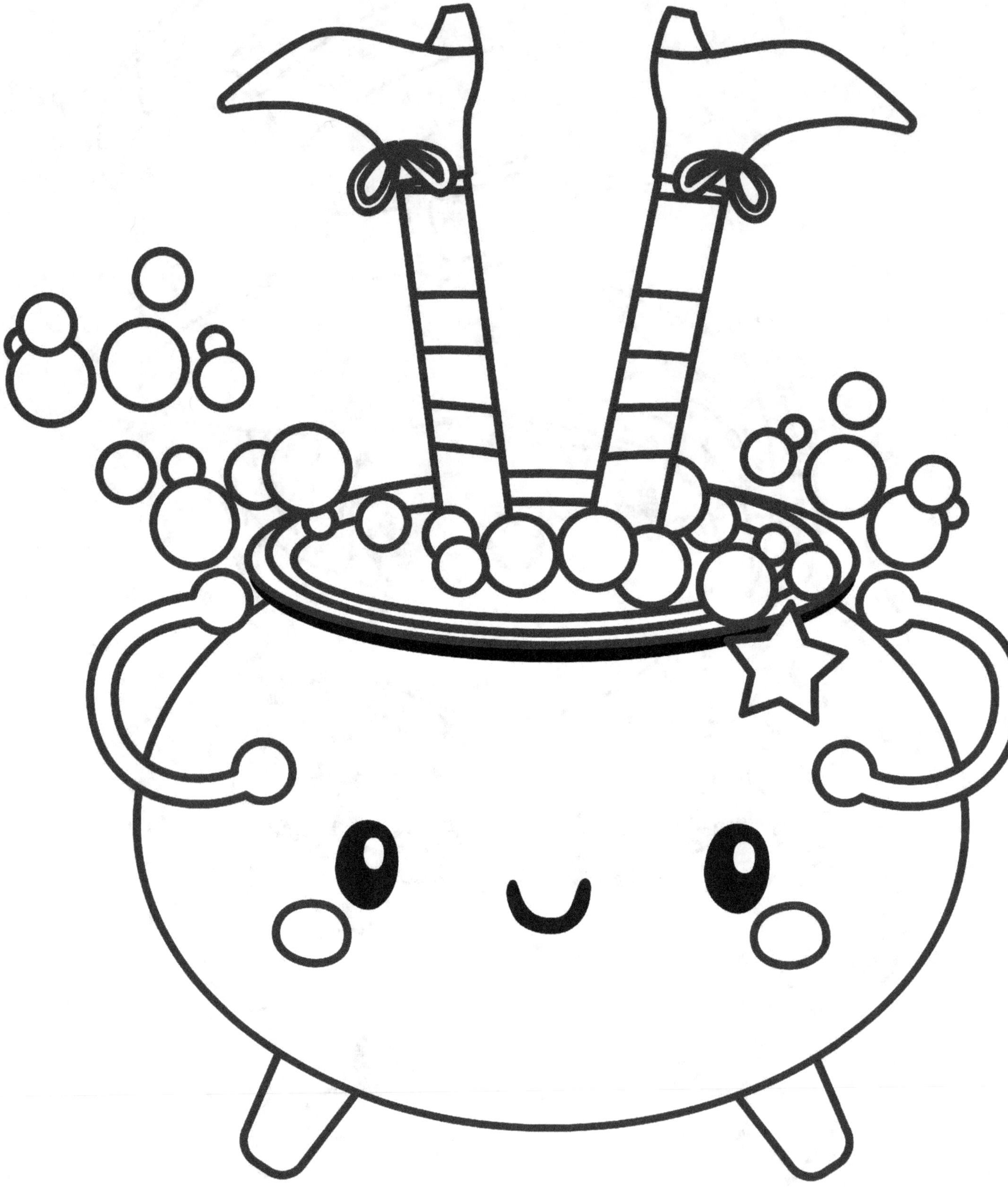

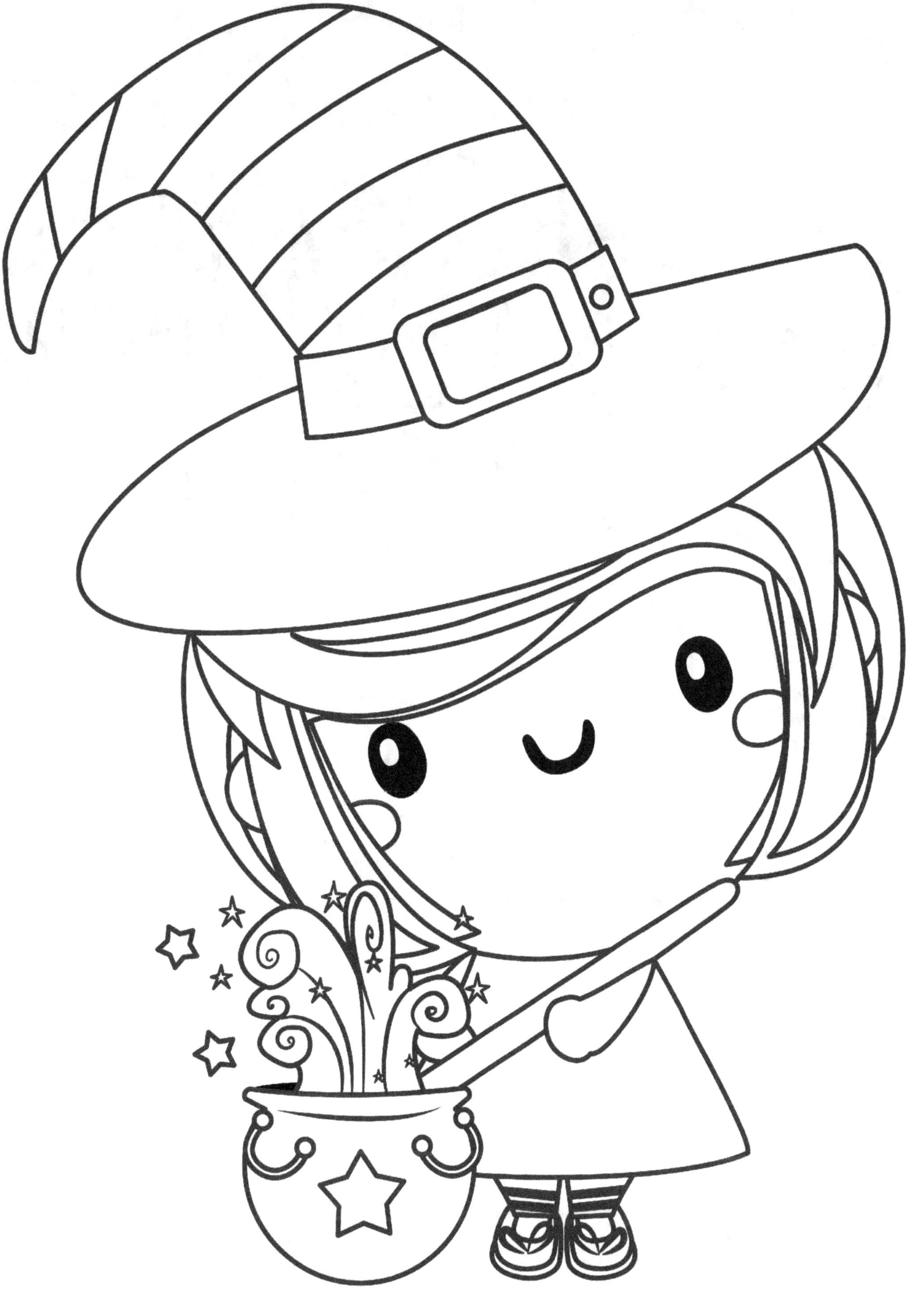

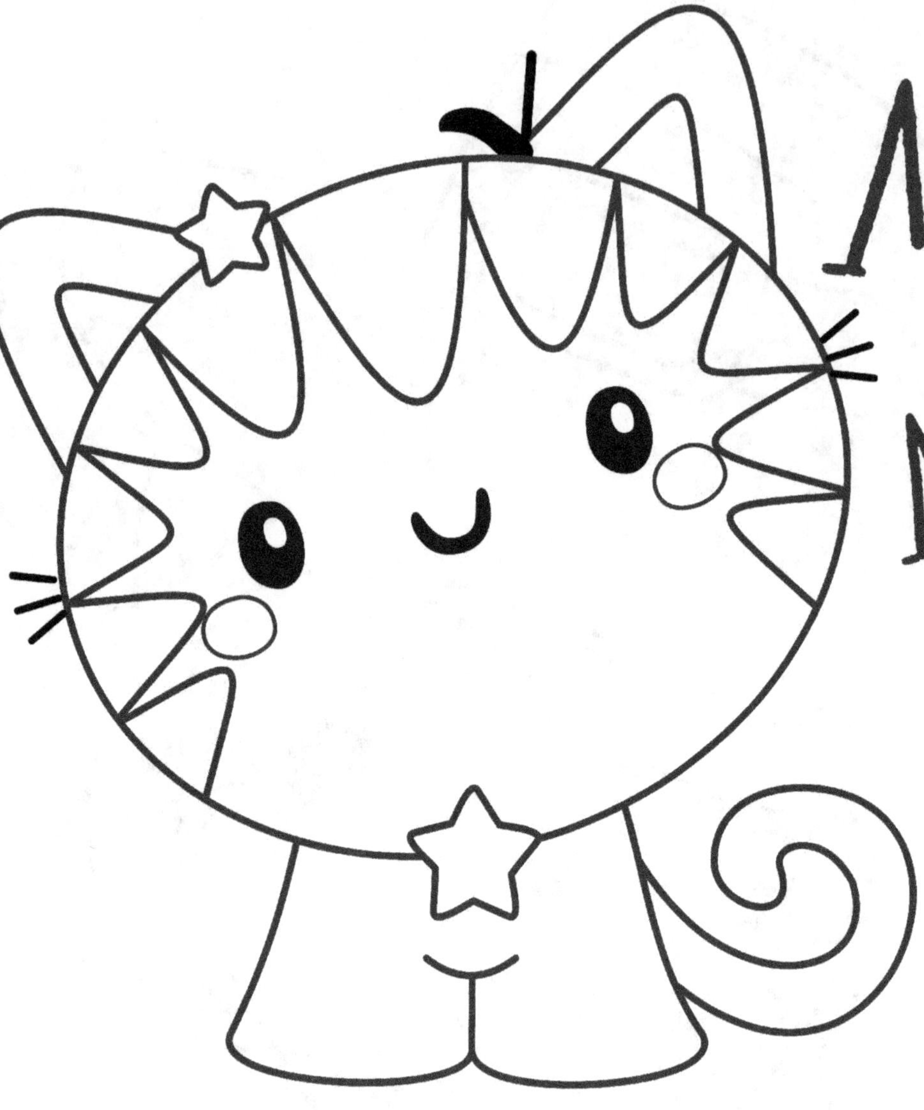

Meow
Meow

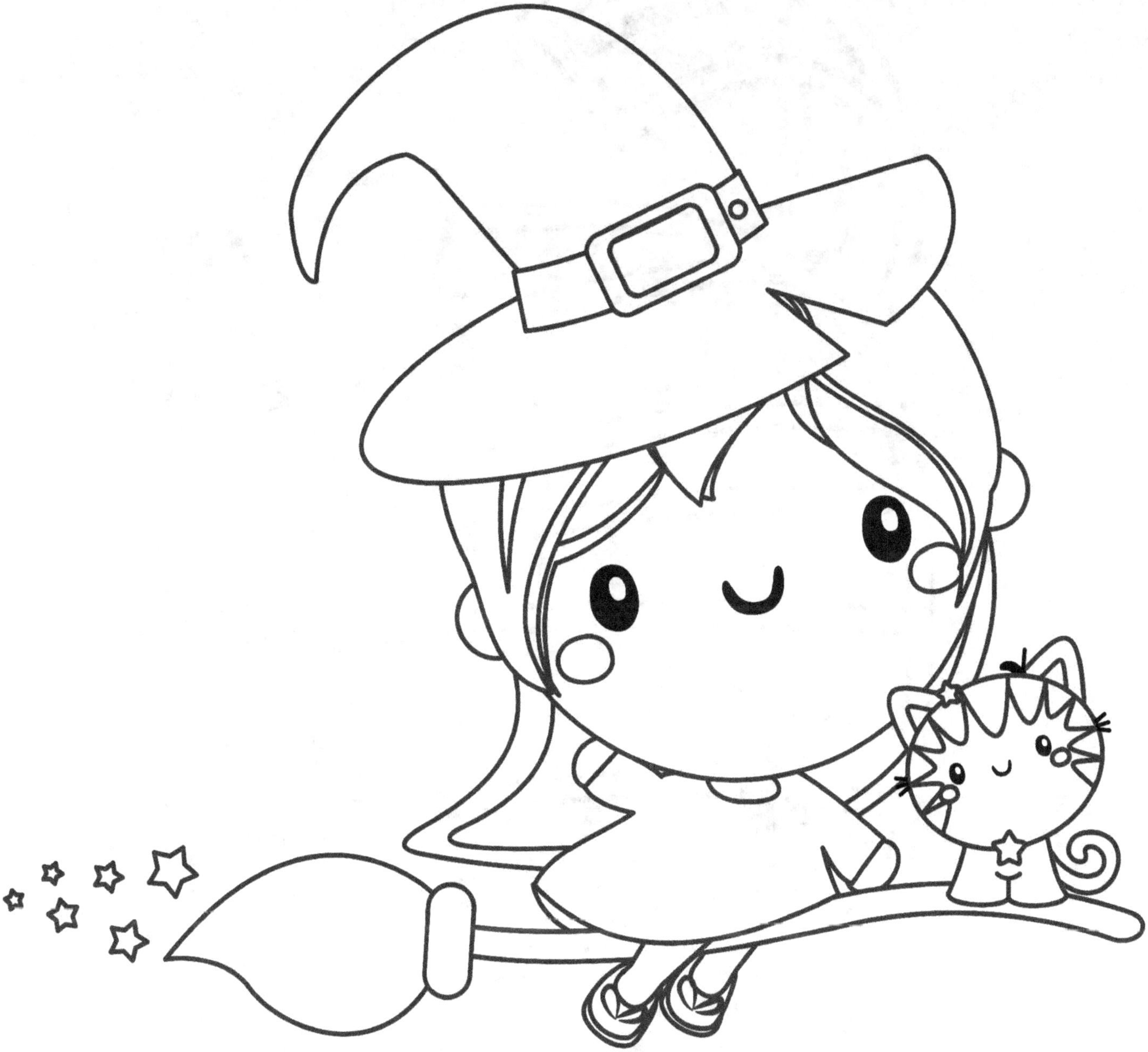

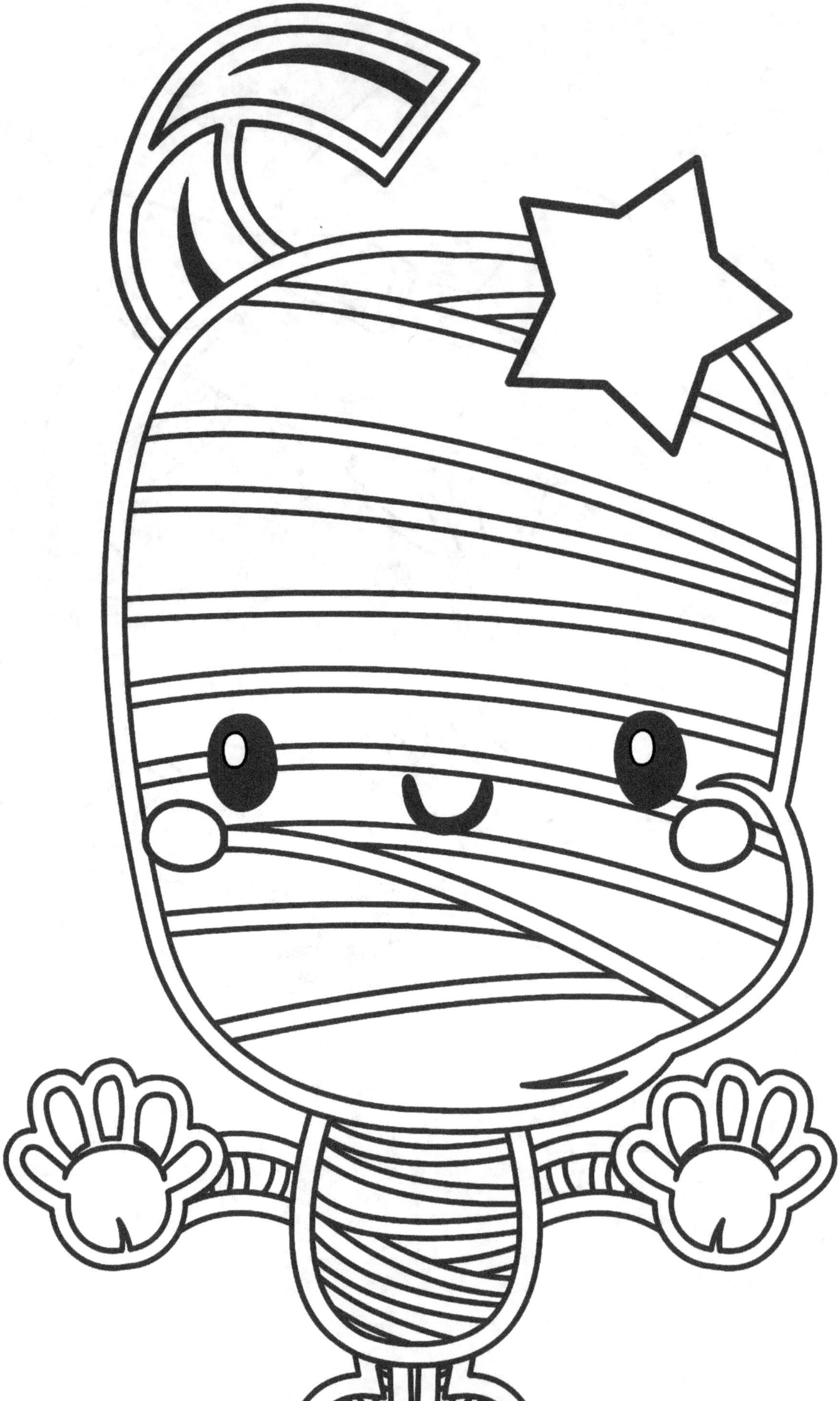

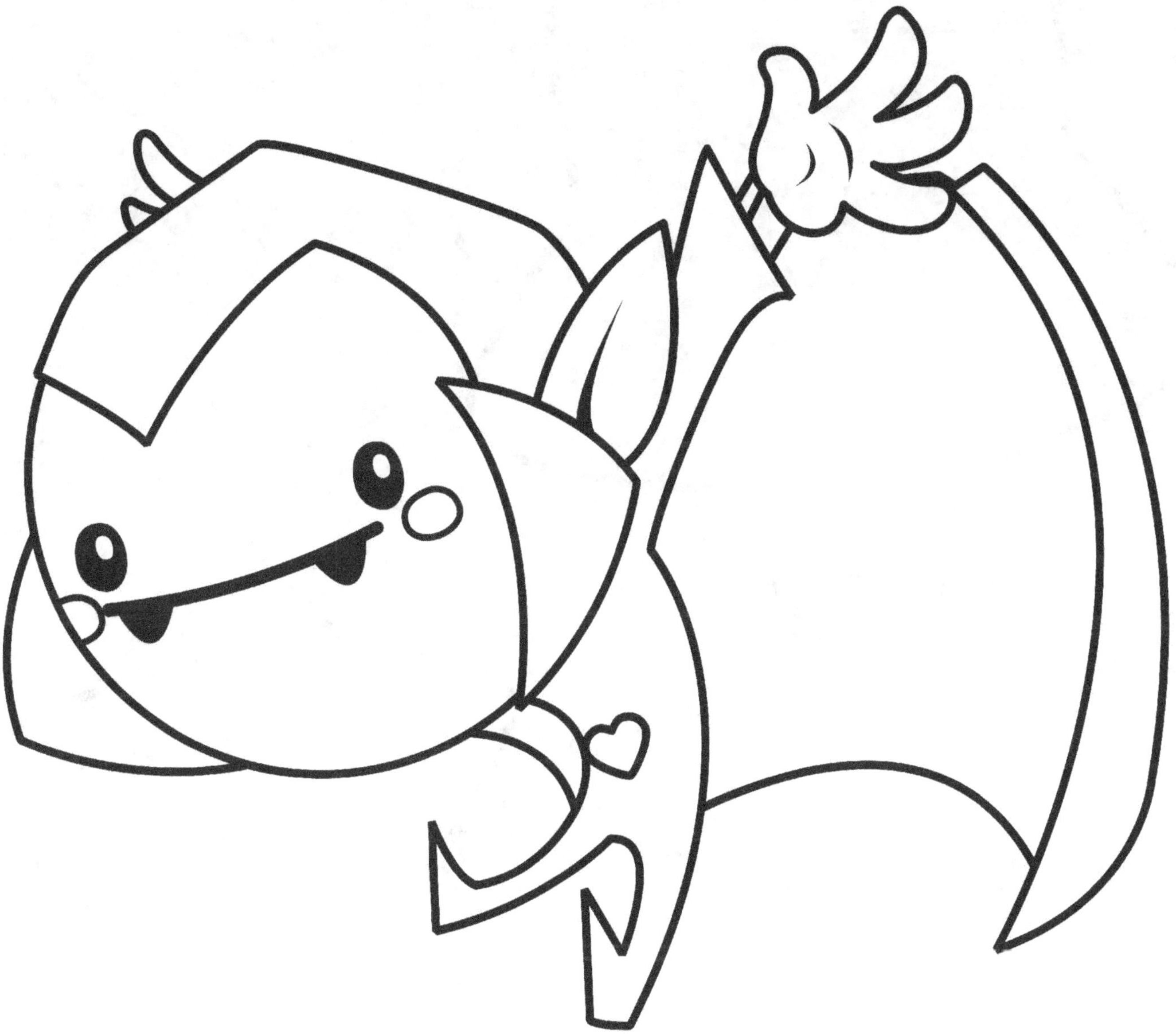

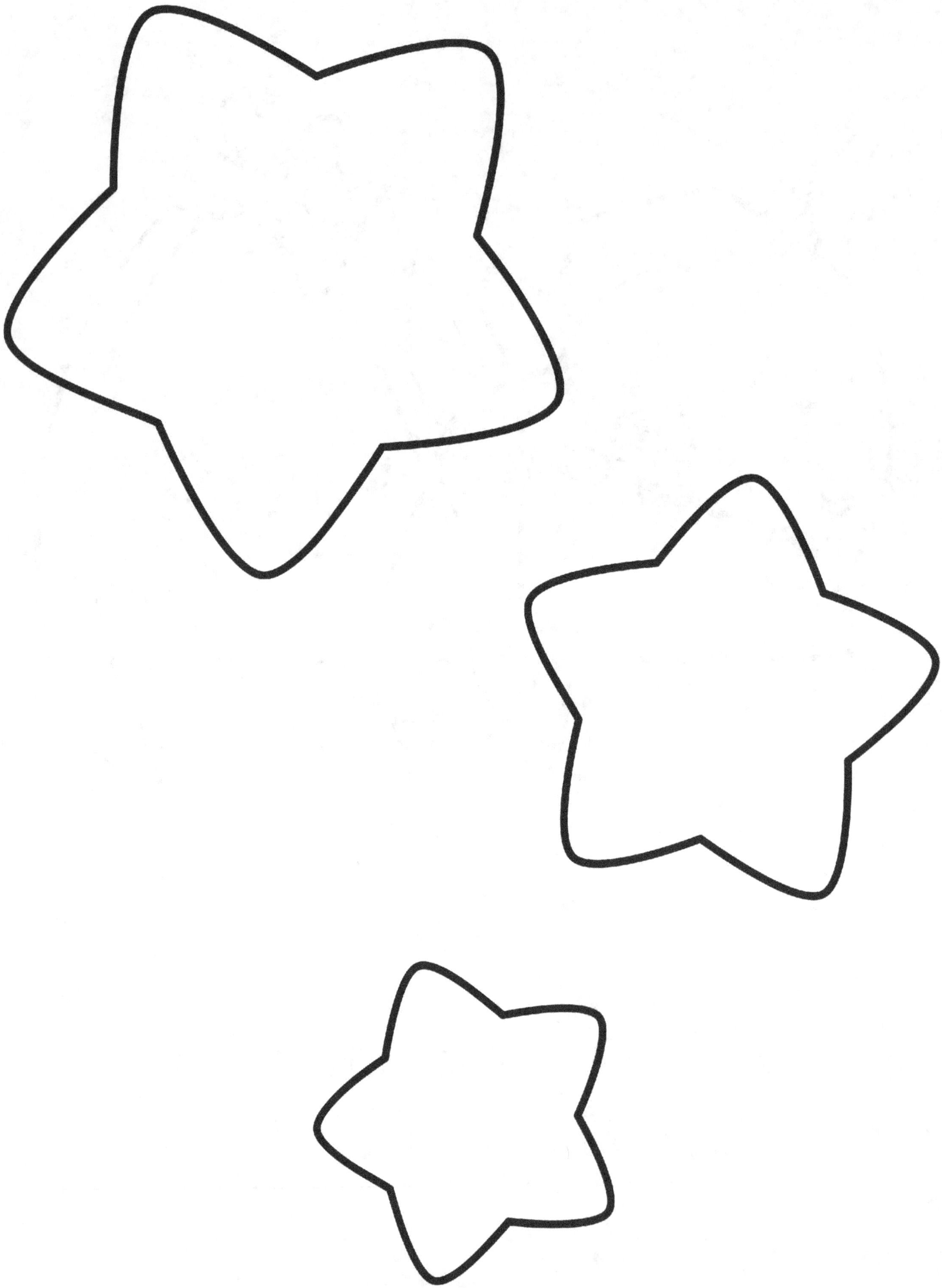

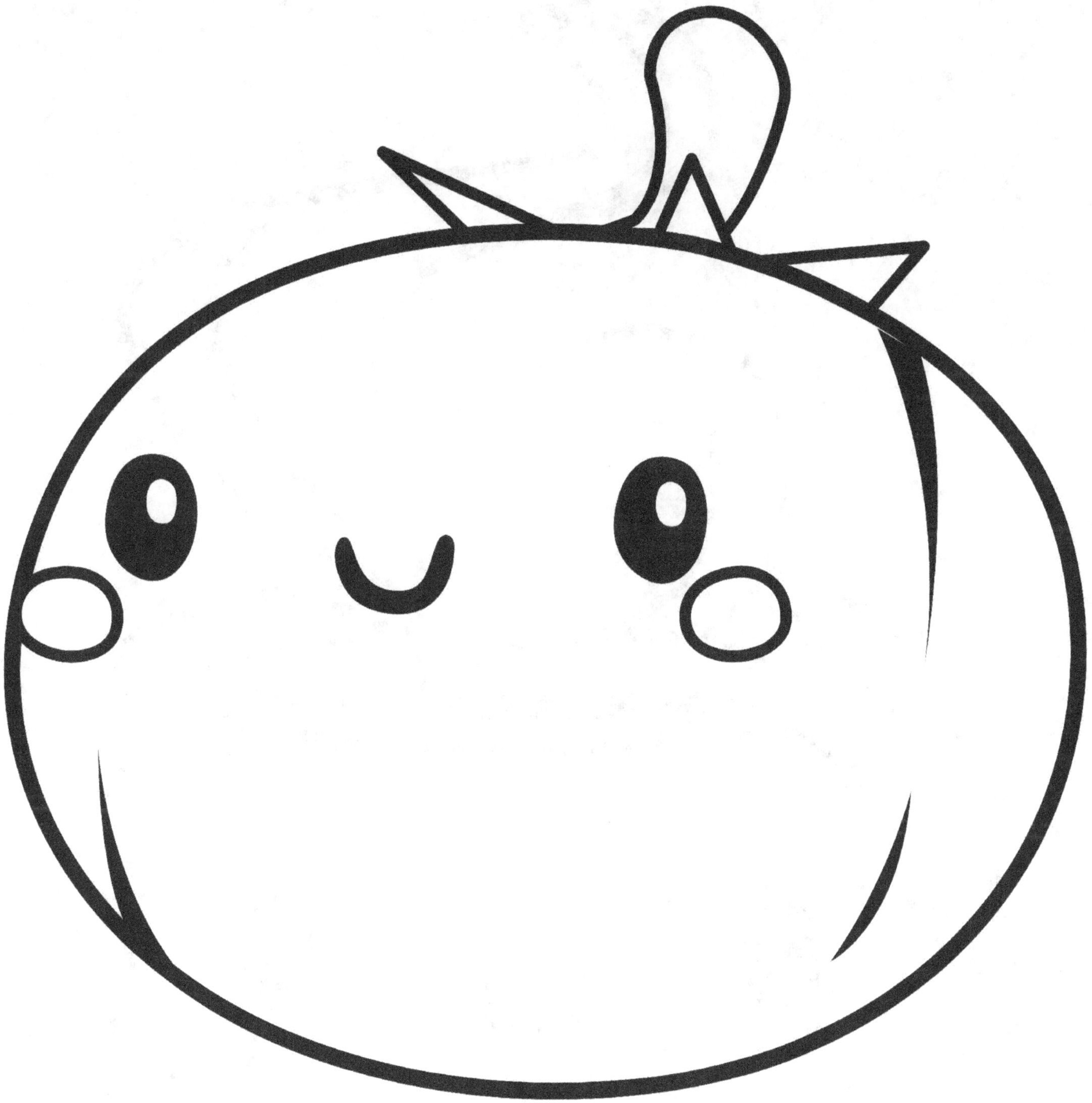

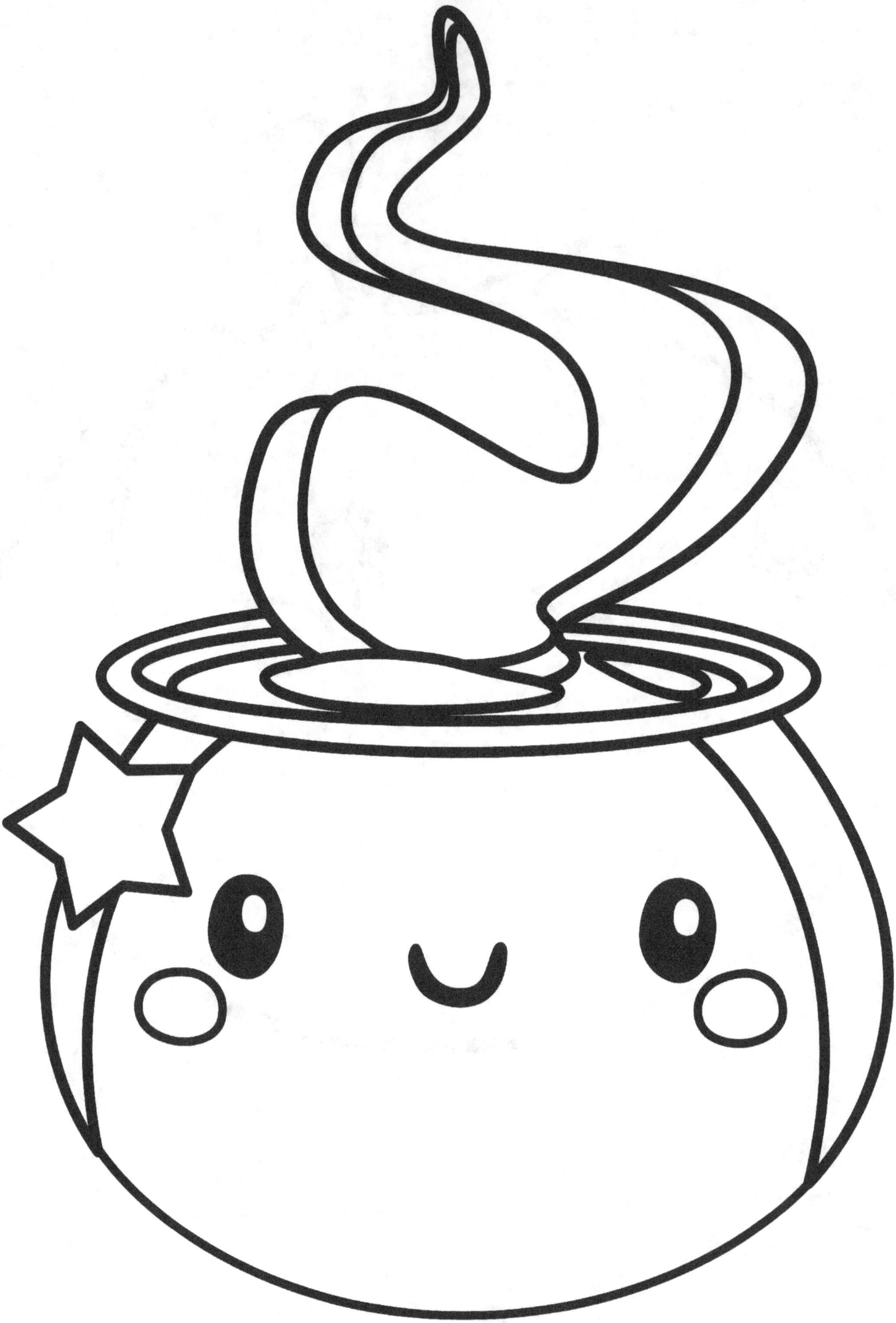

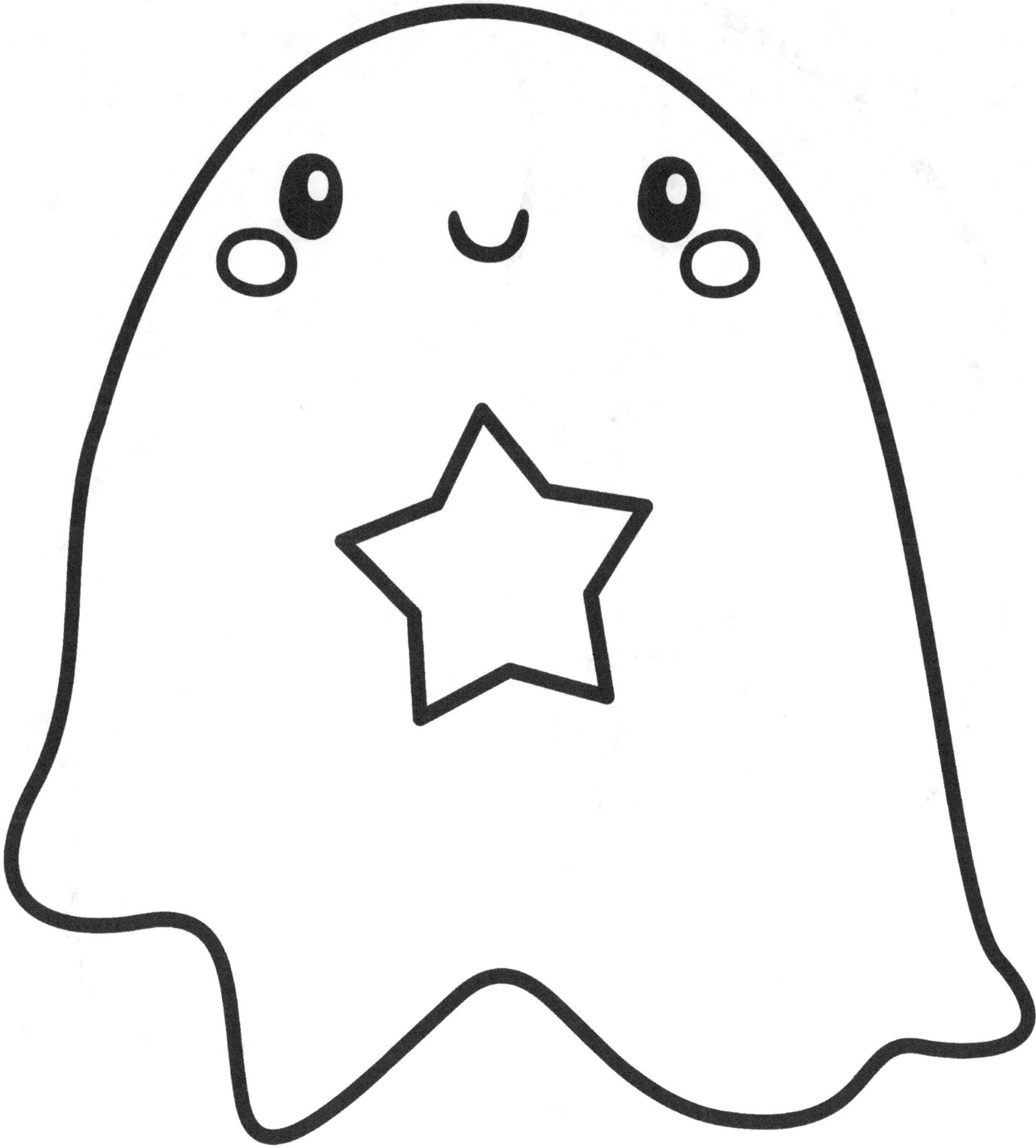

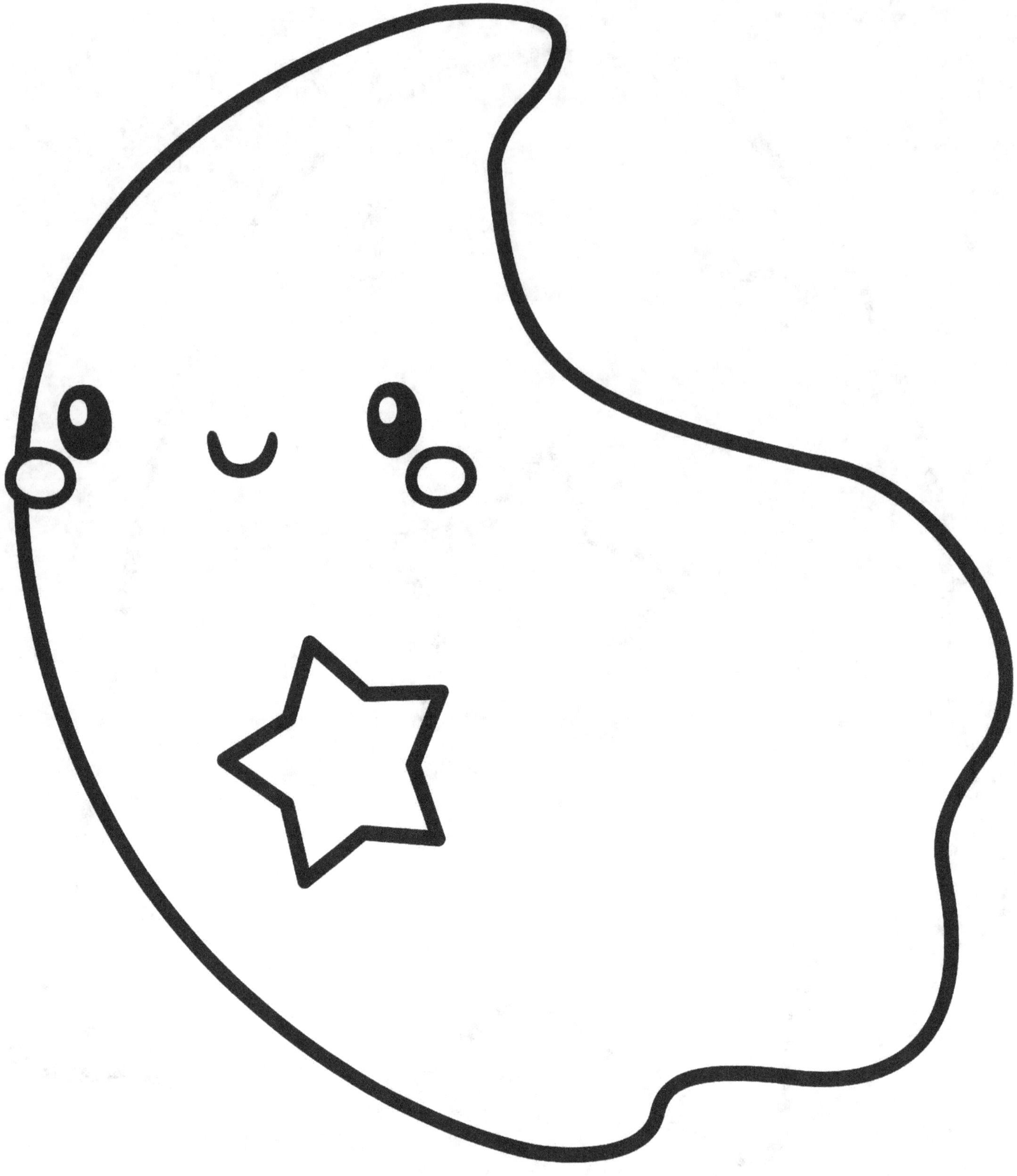

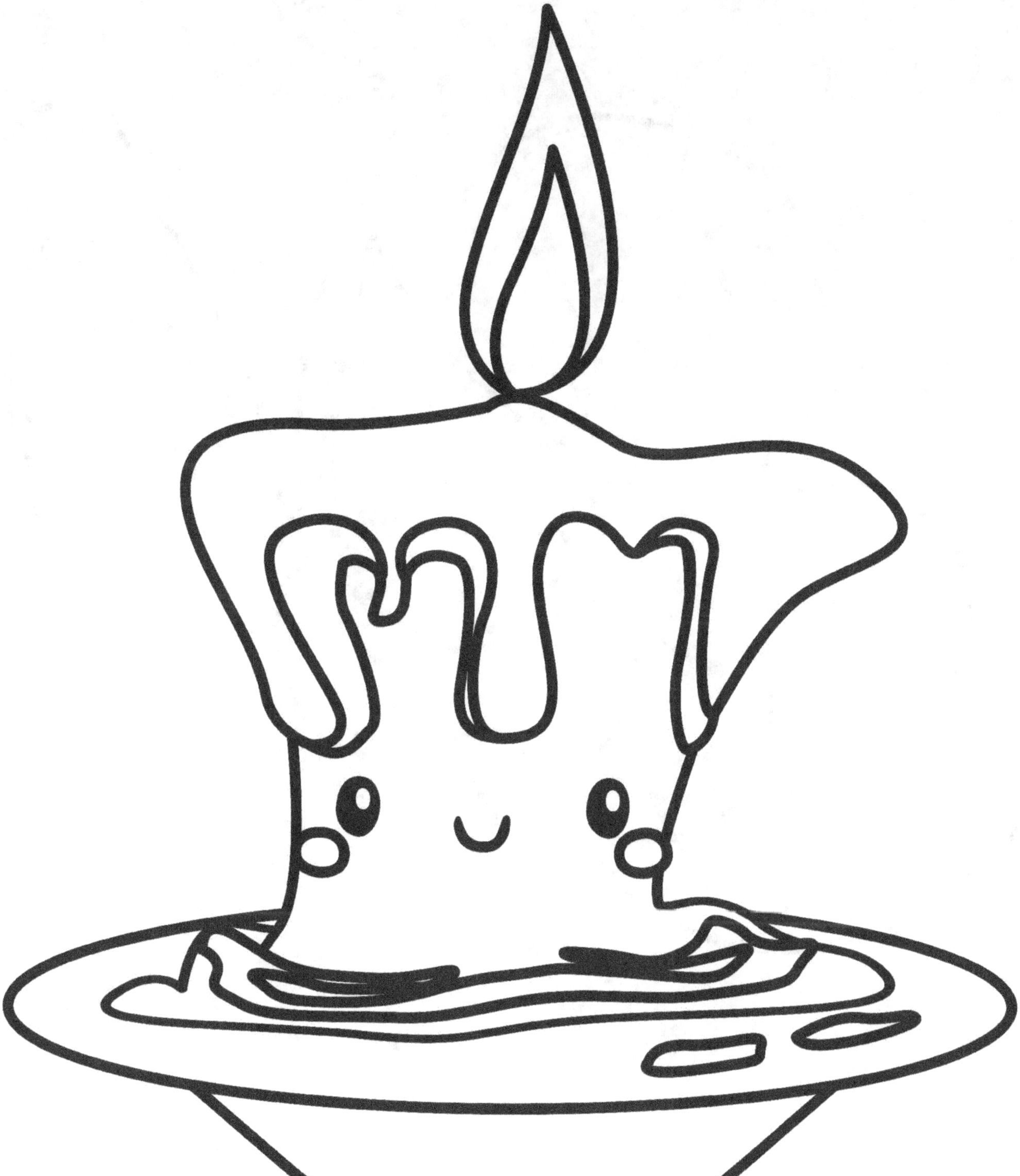

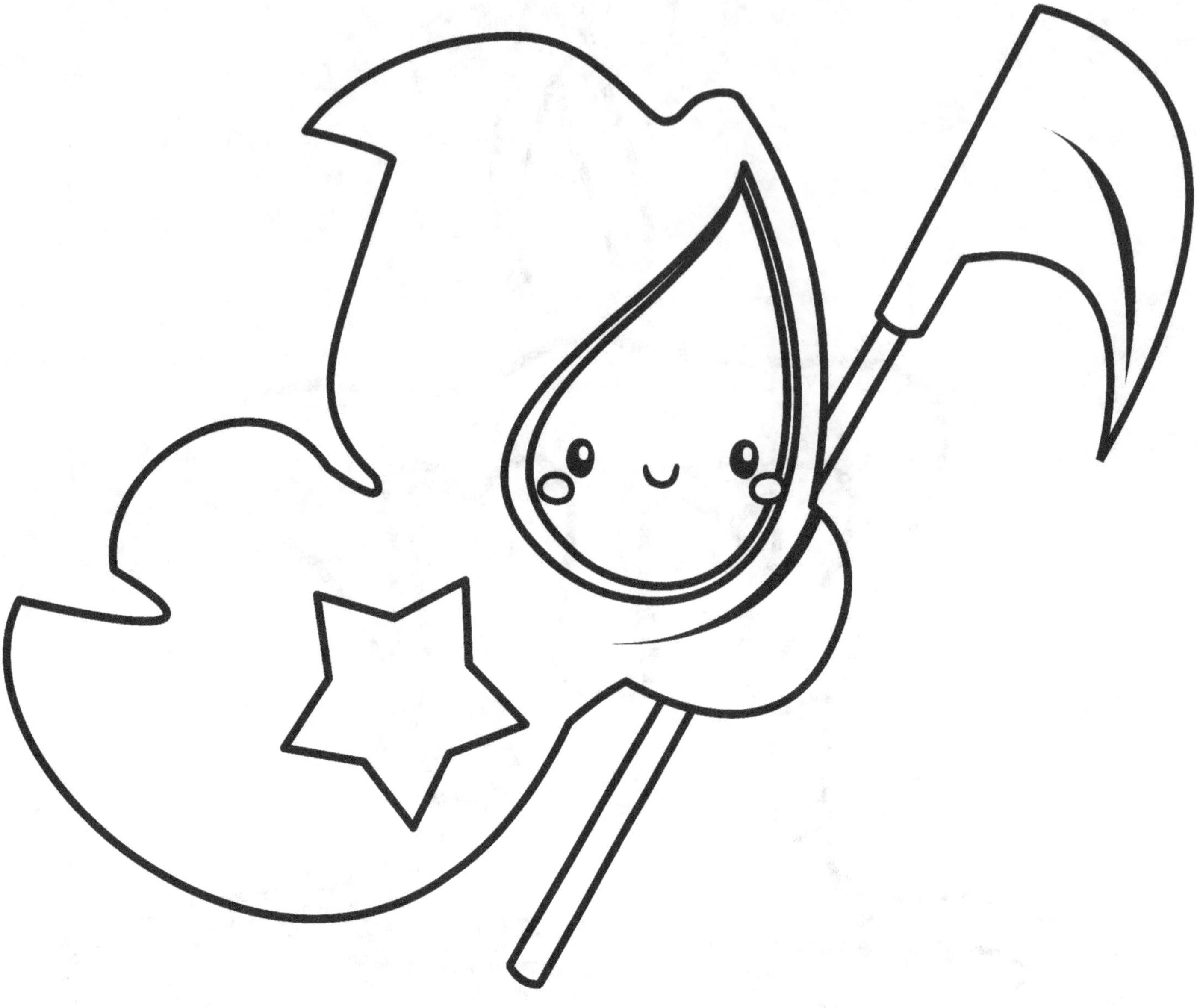

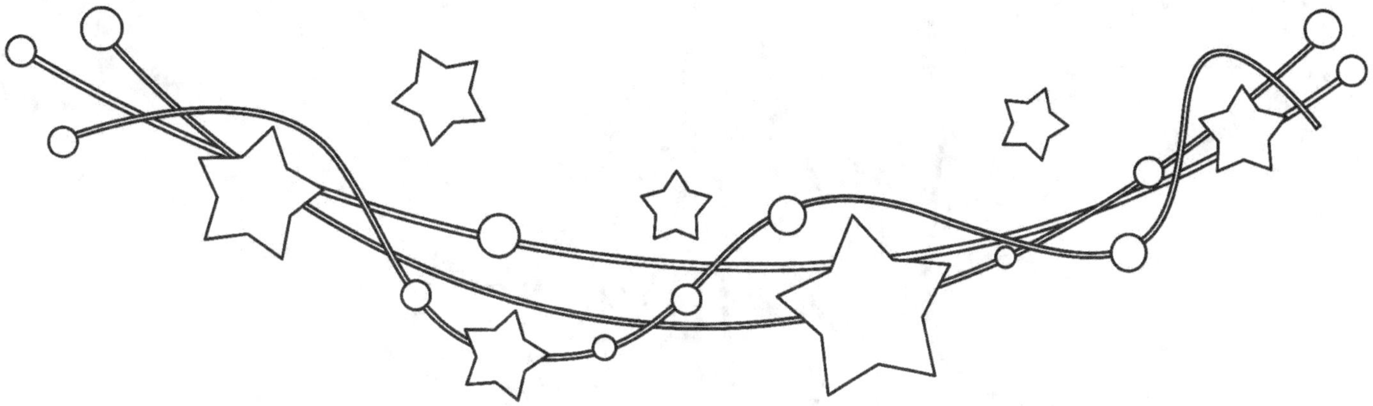

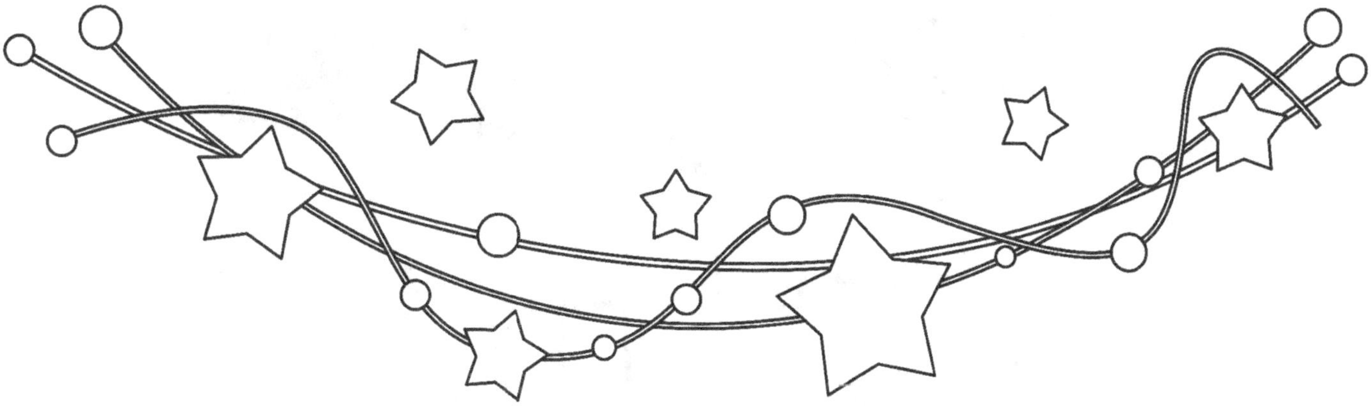

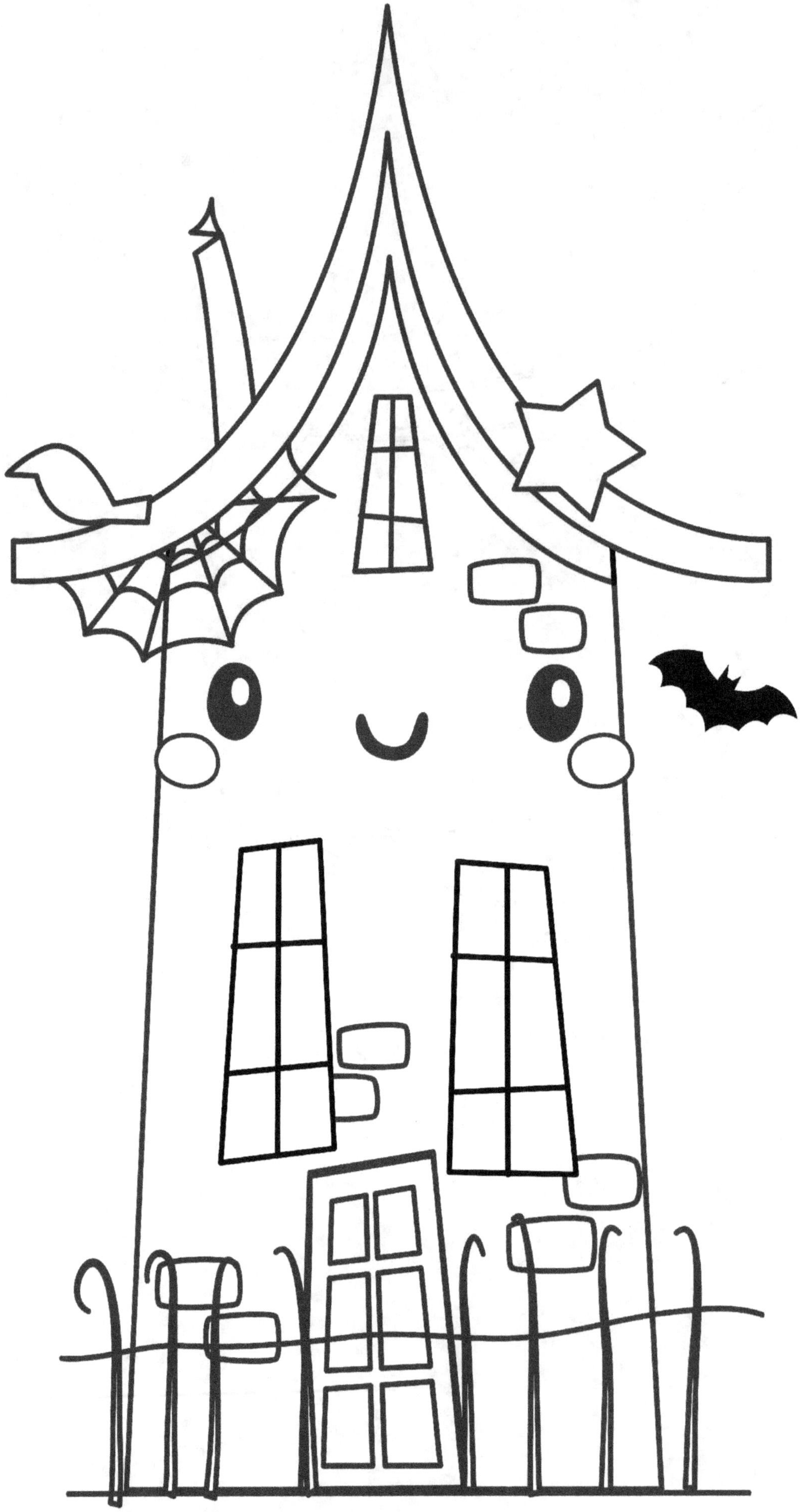

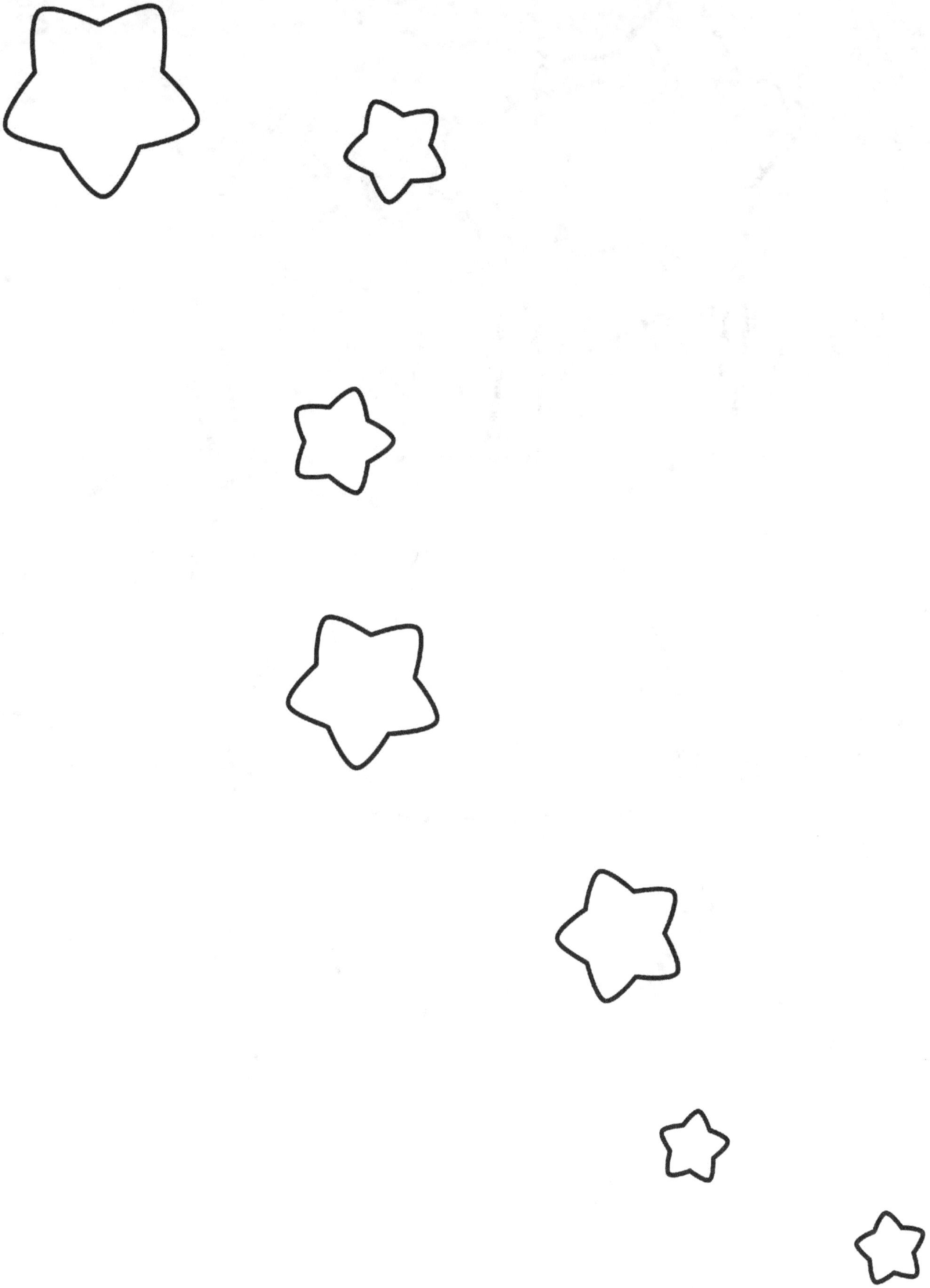

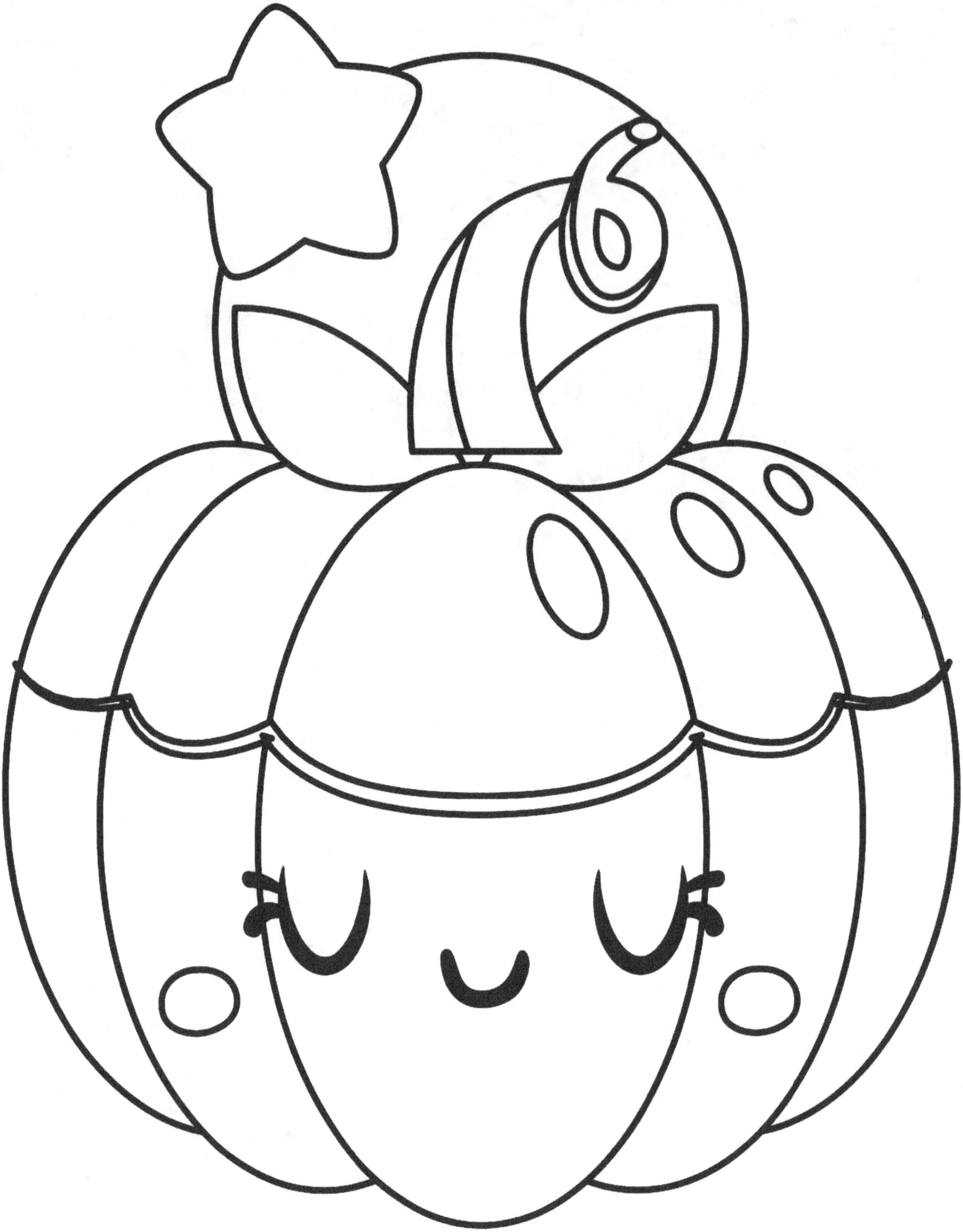

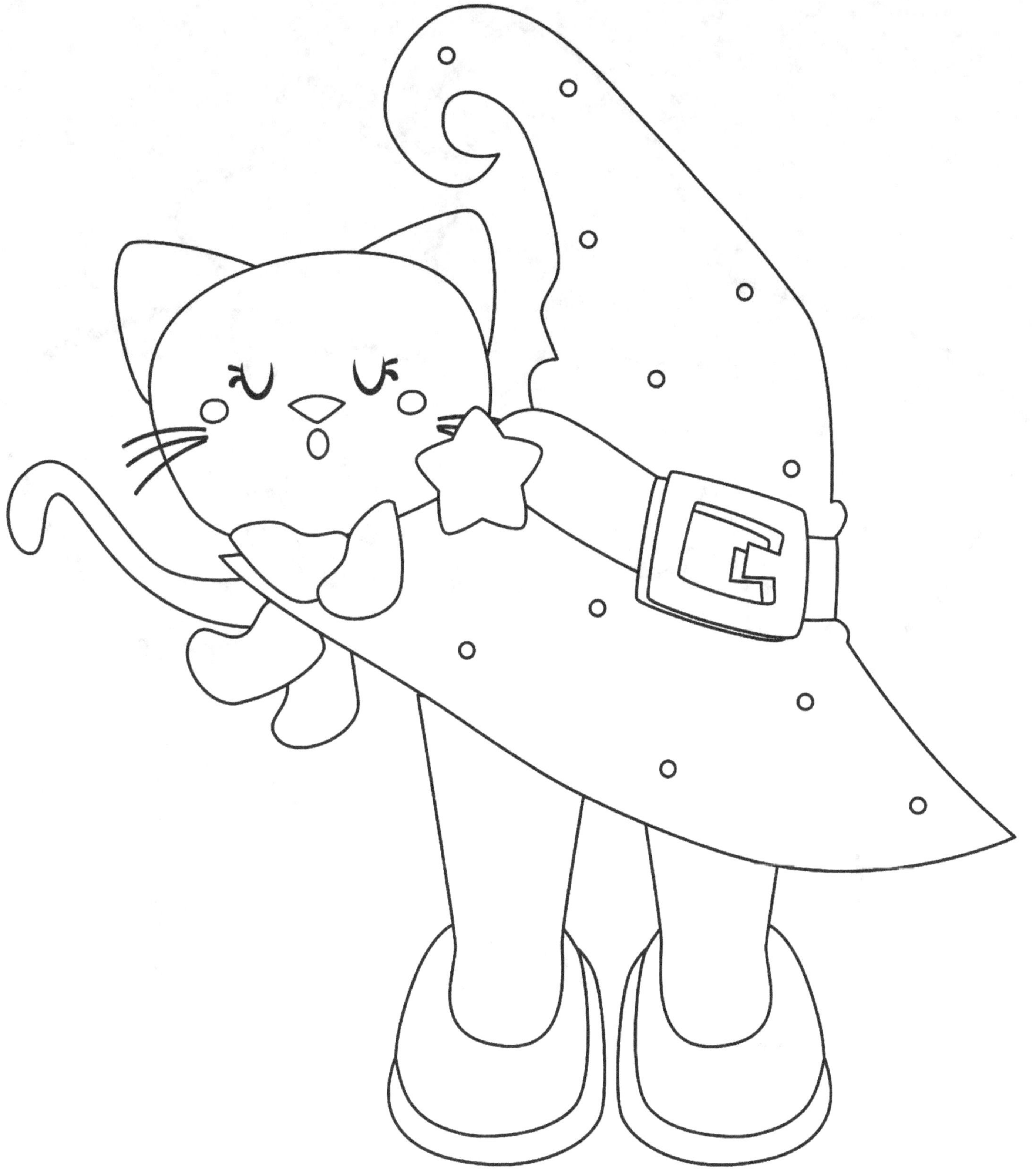

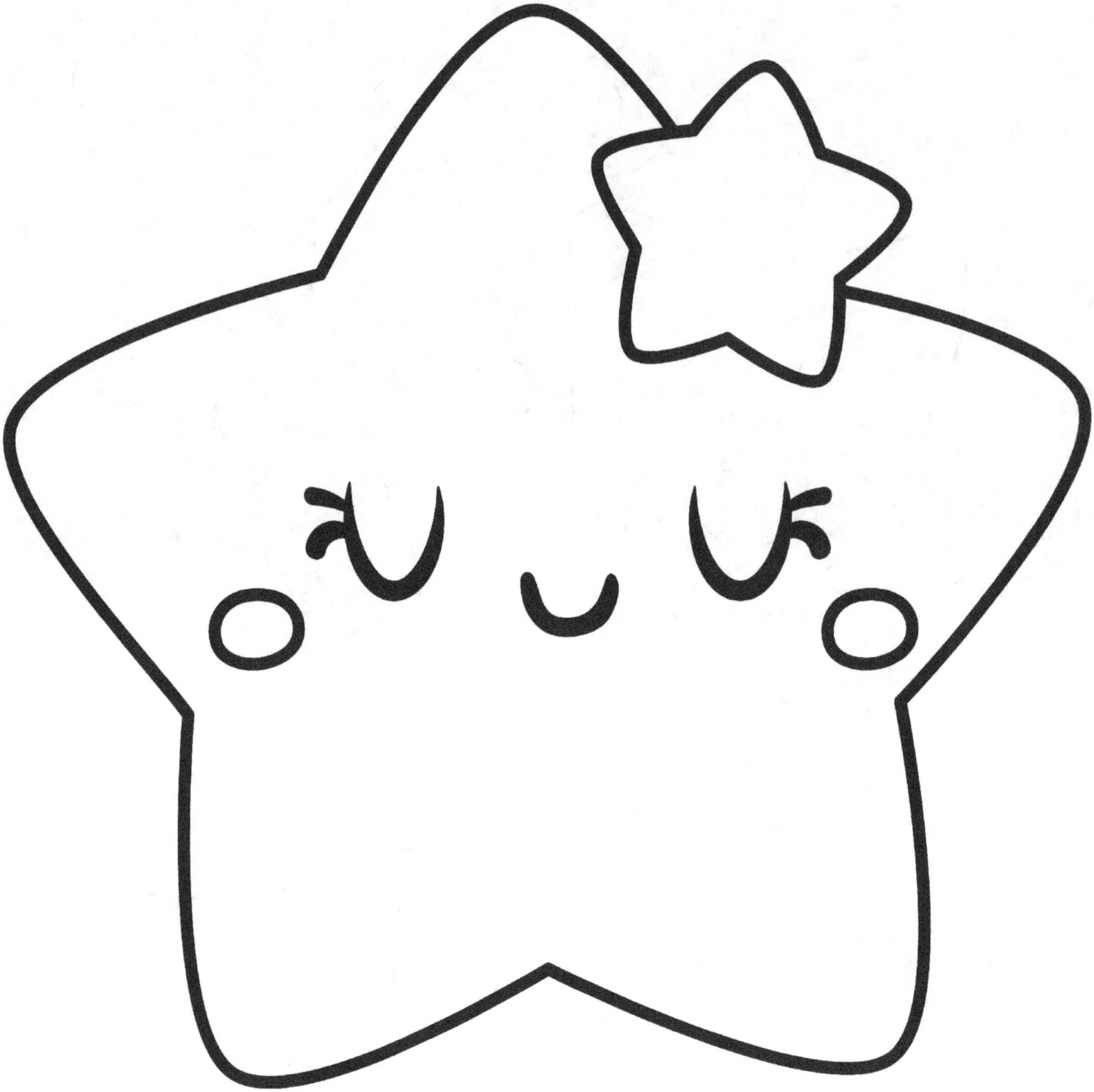

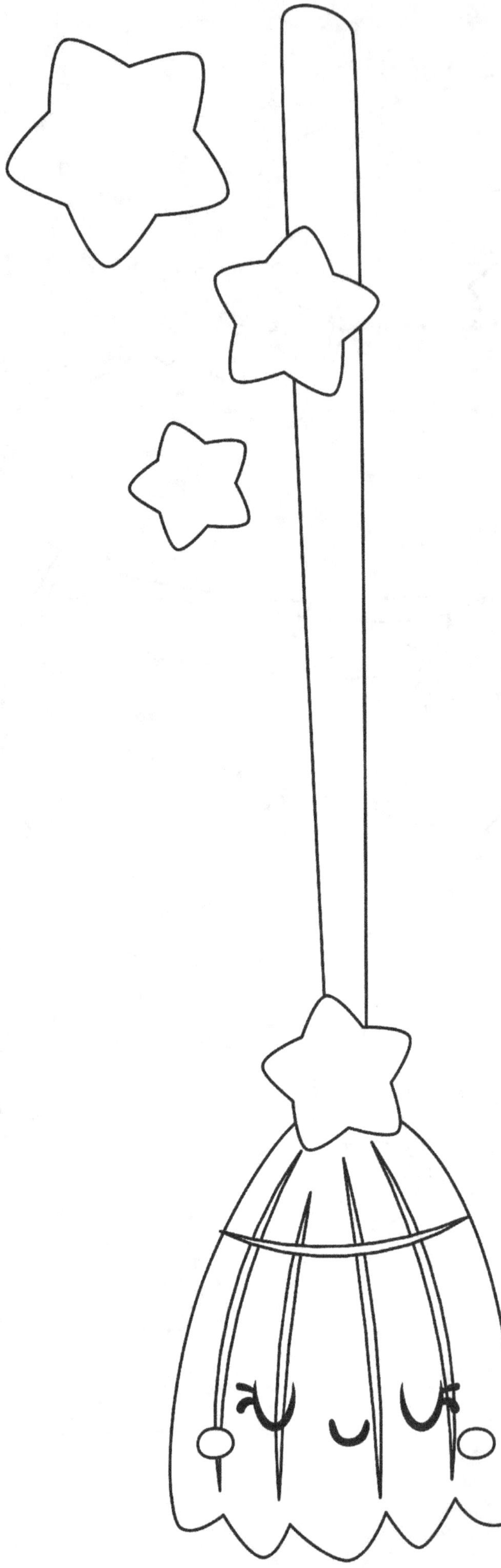

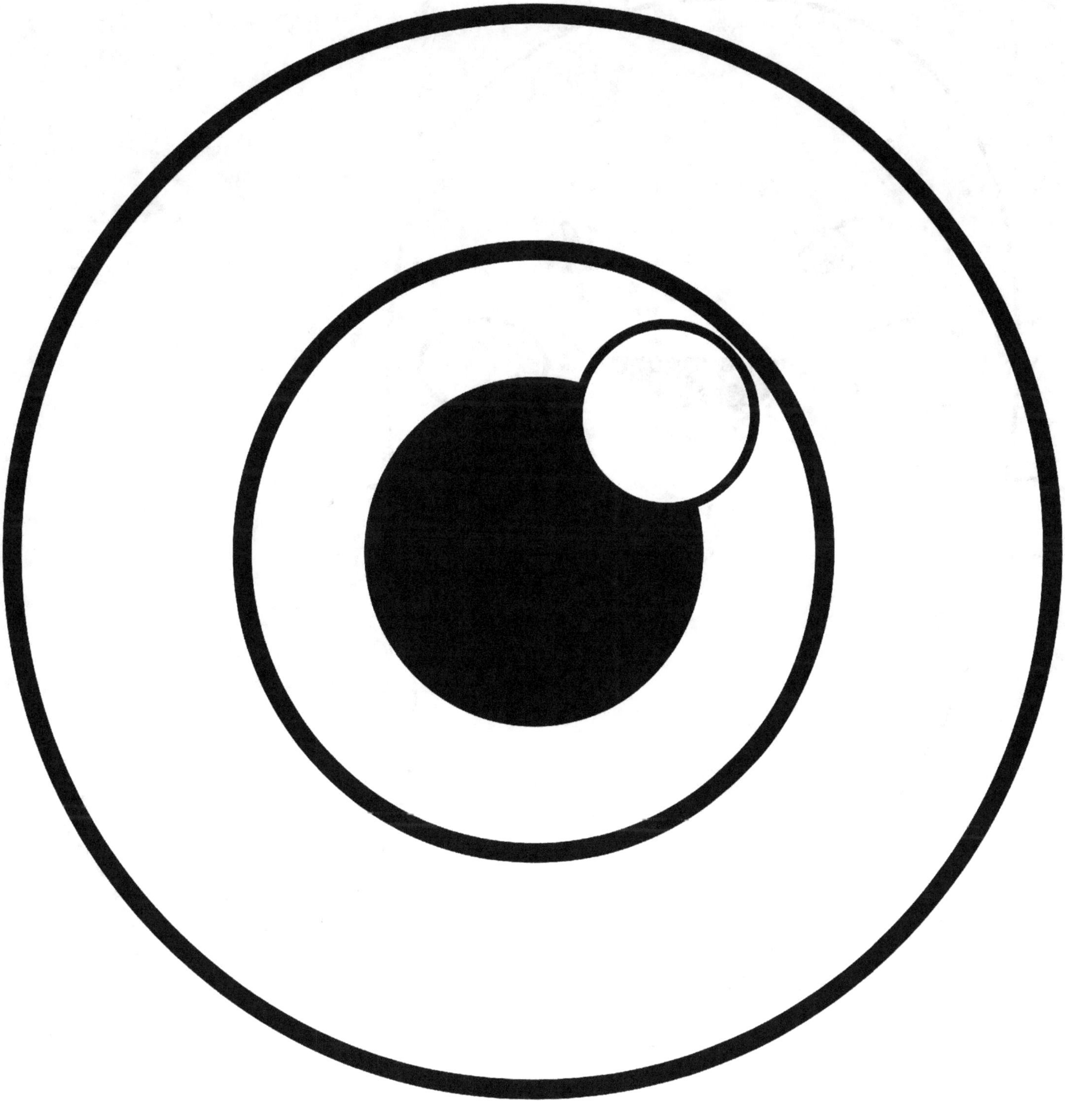

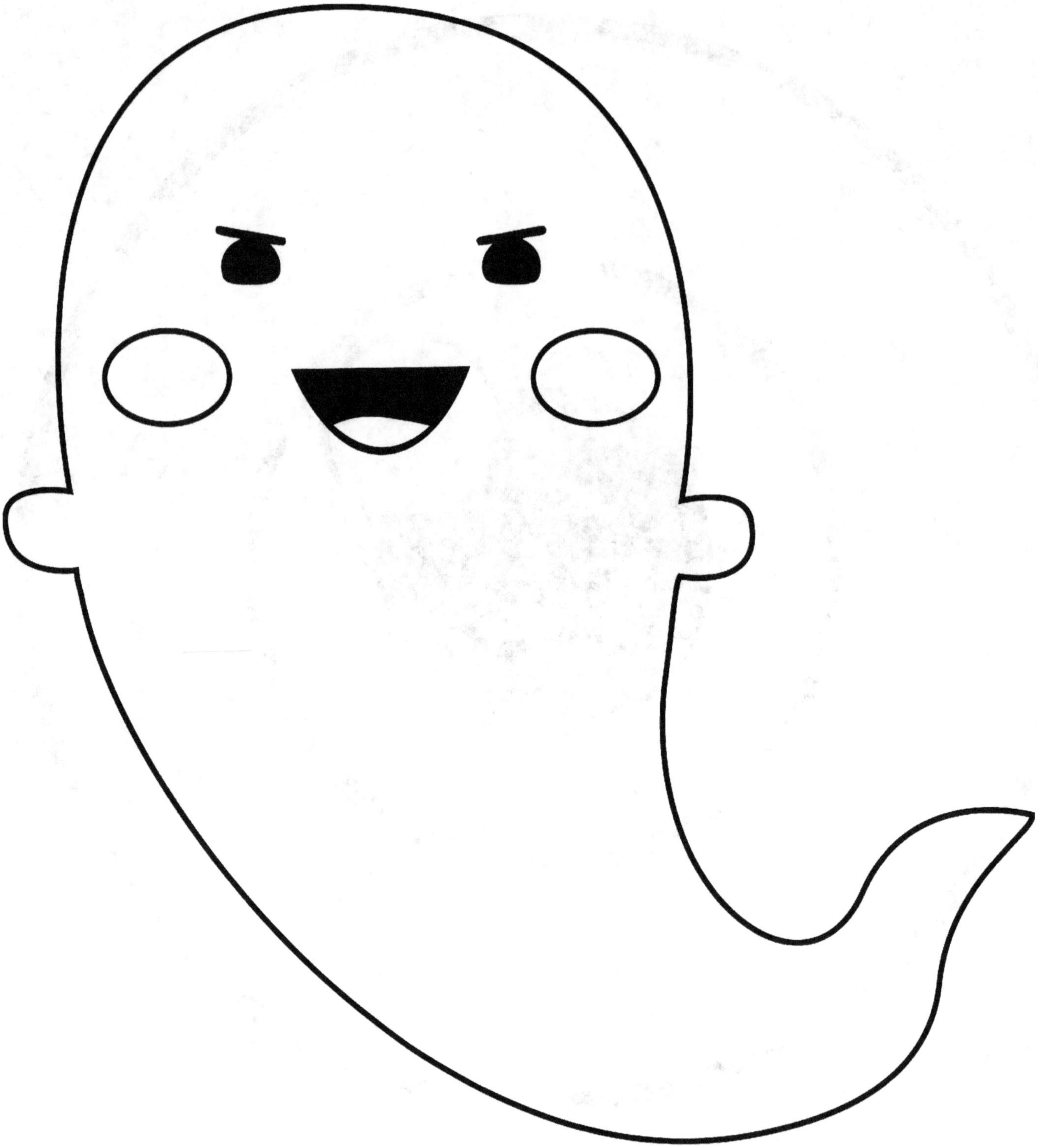

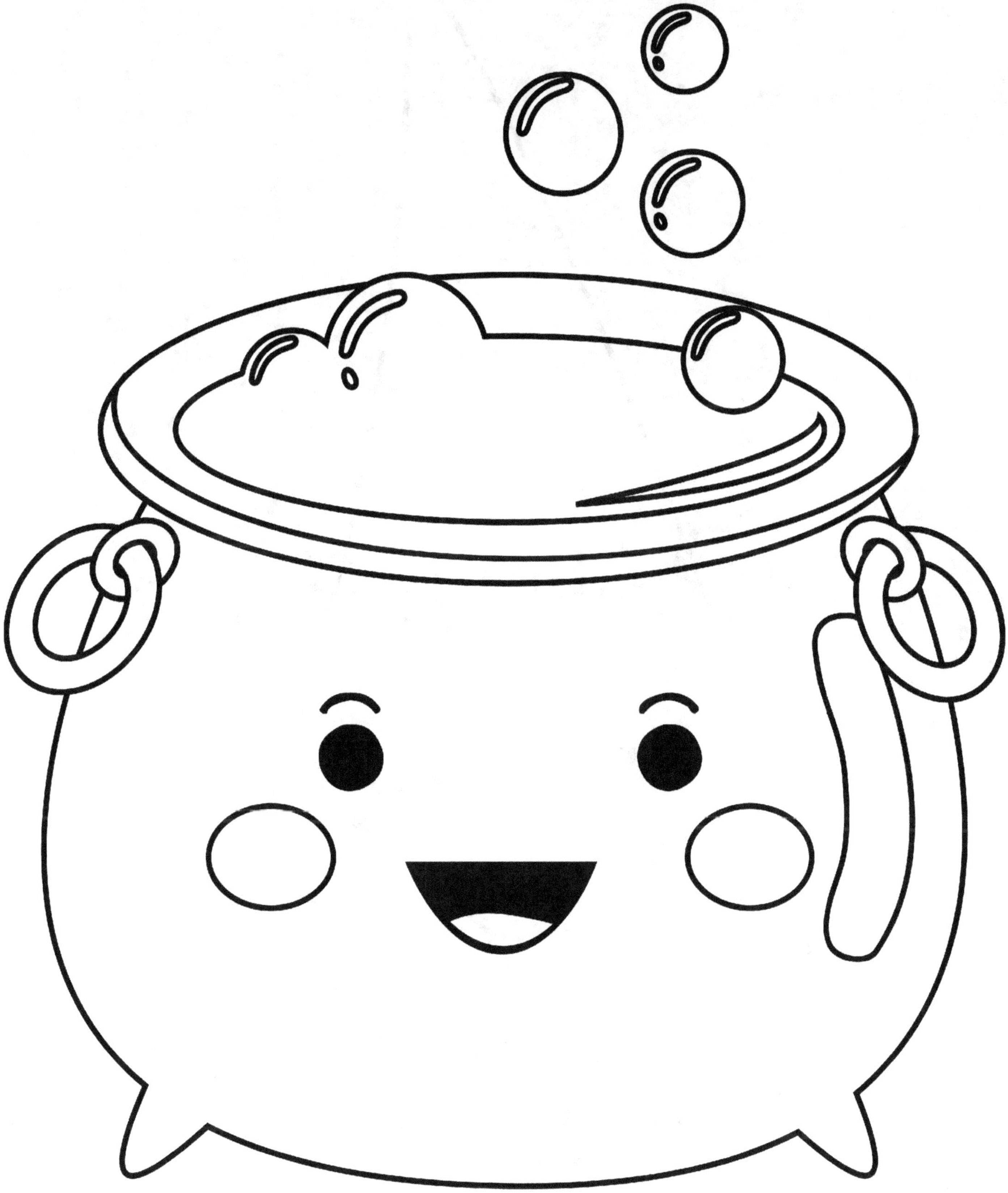

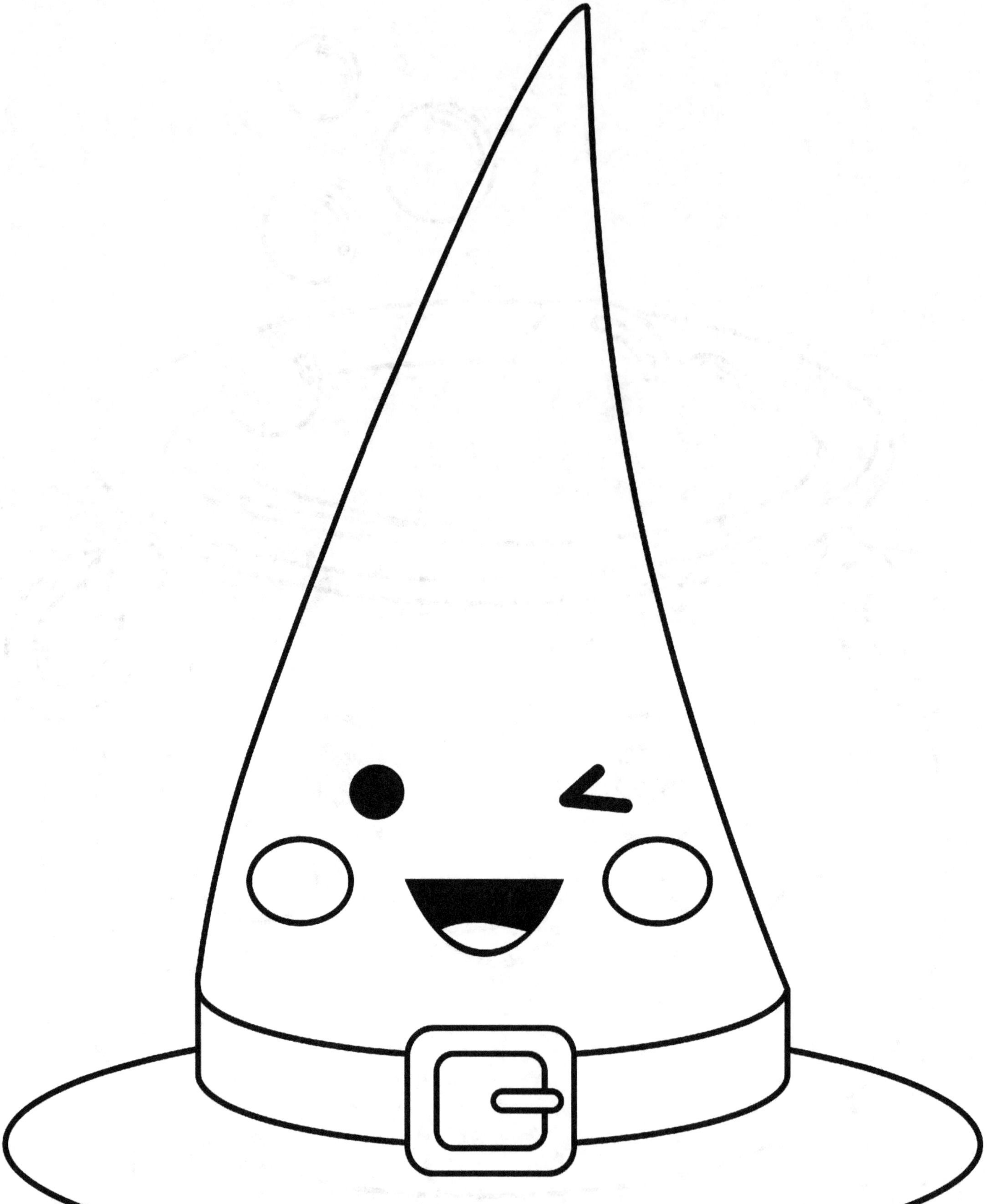

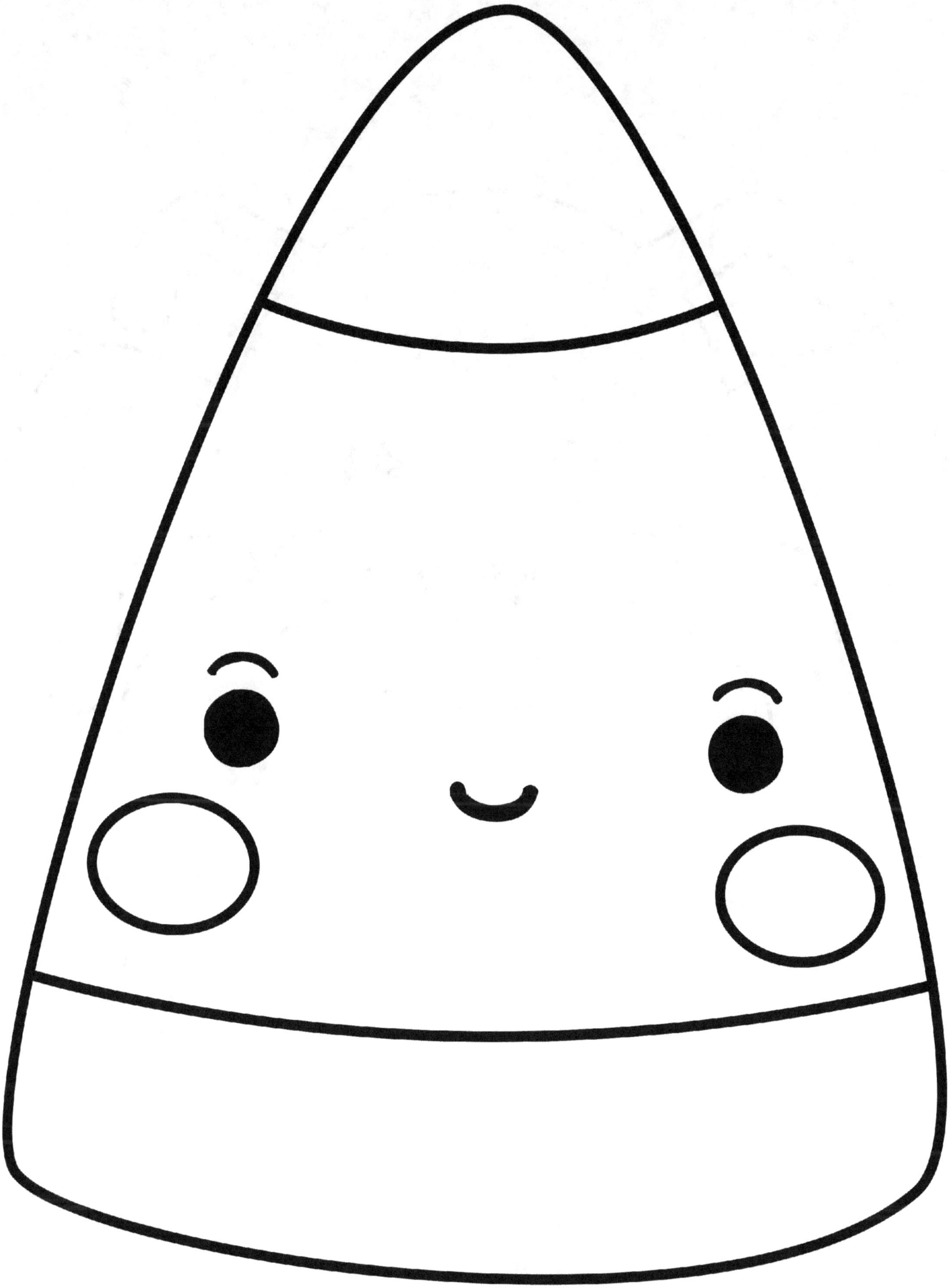

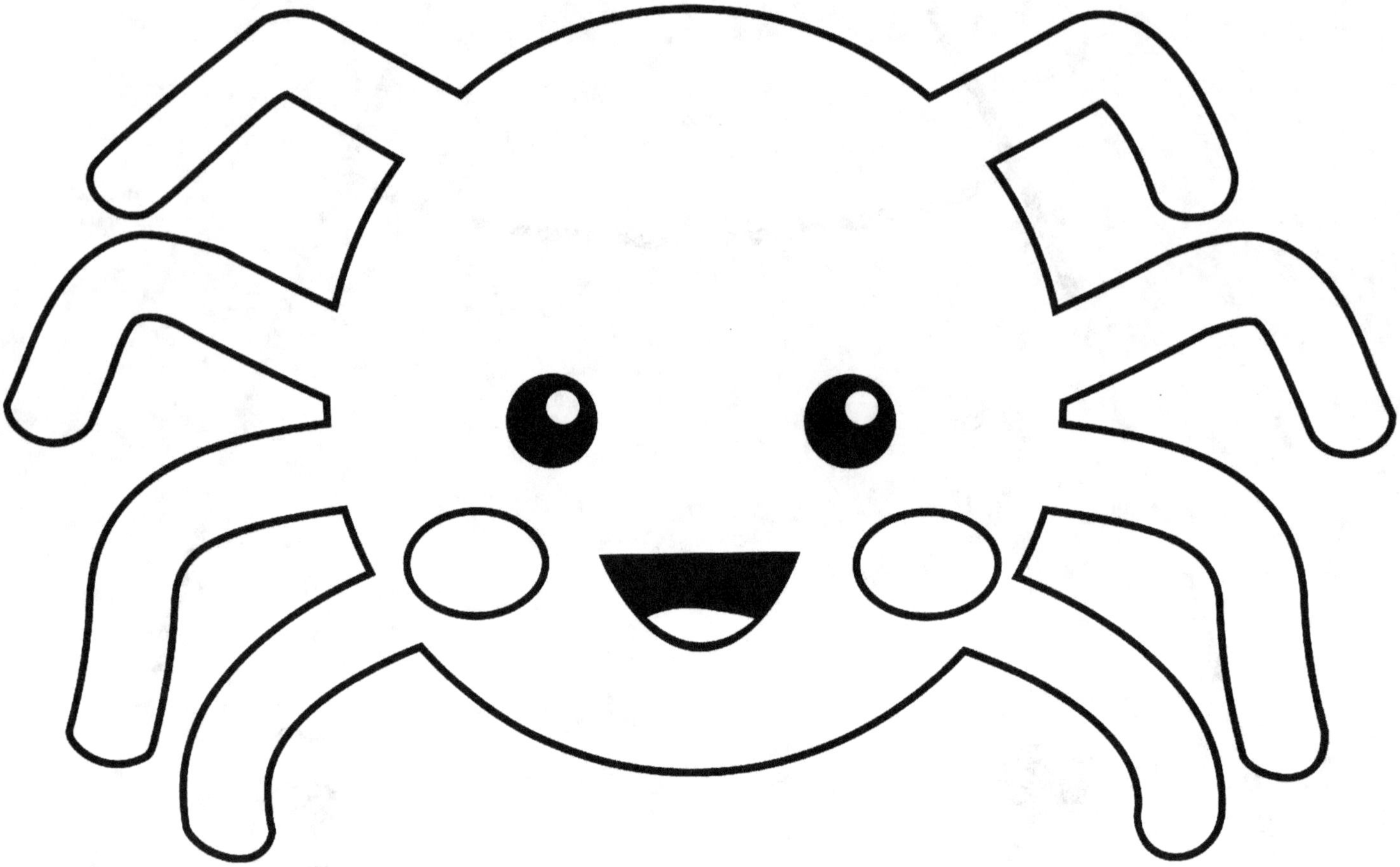

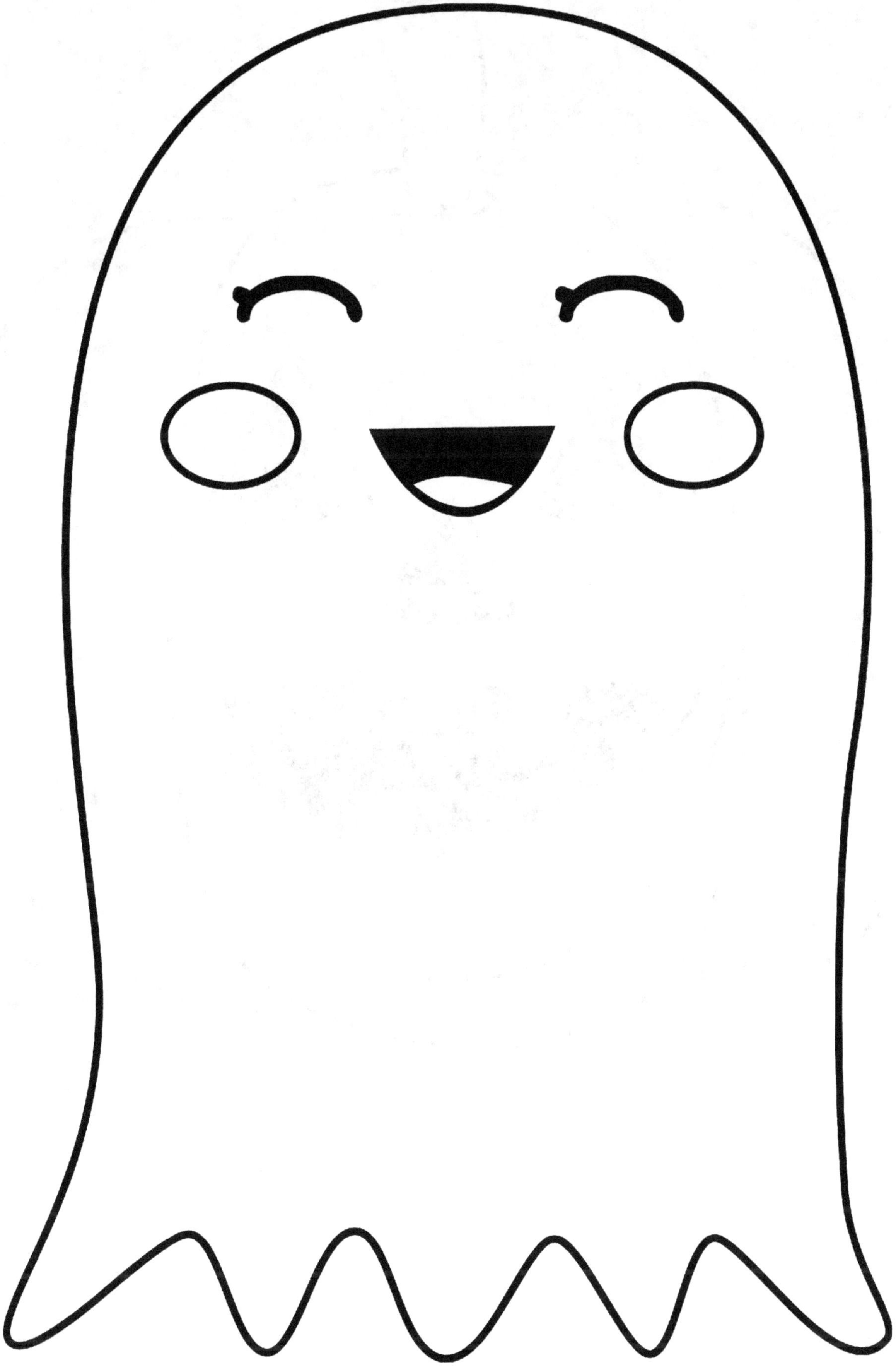

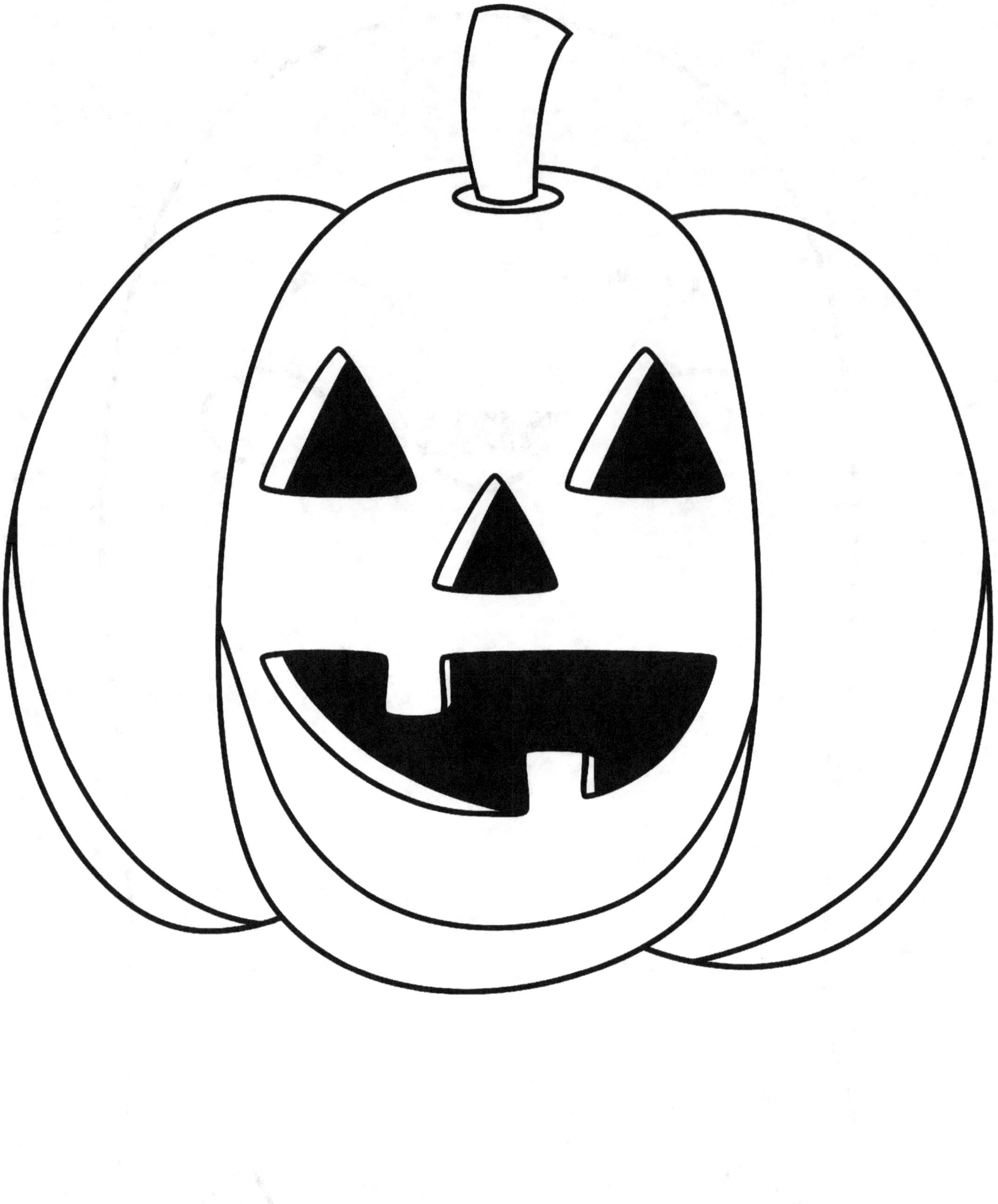

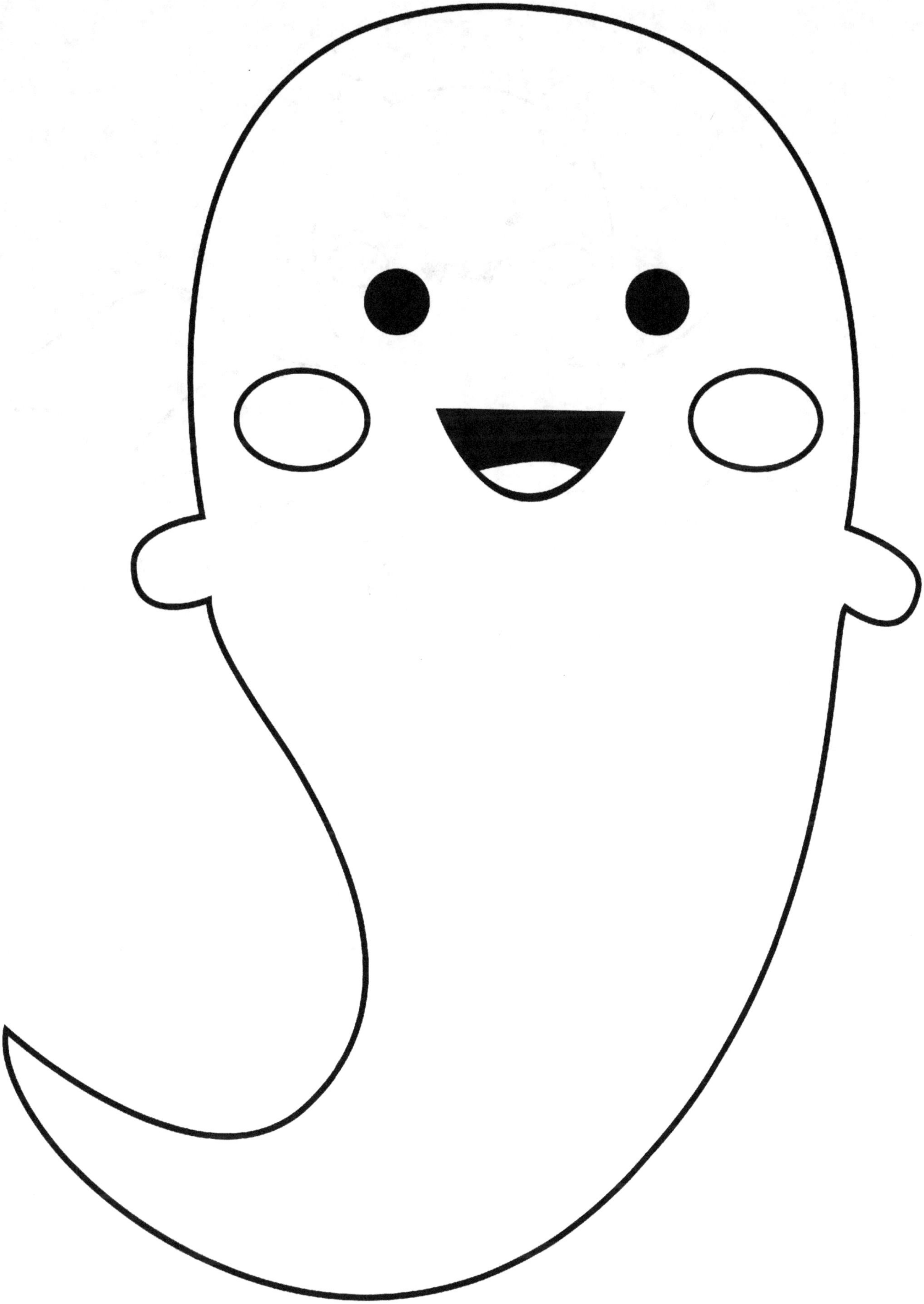

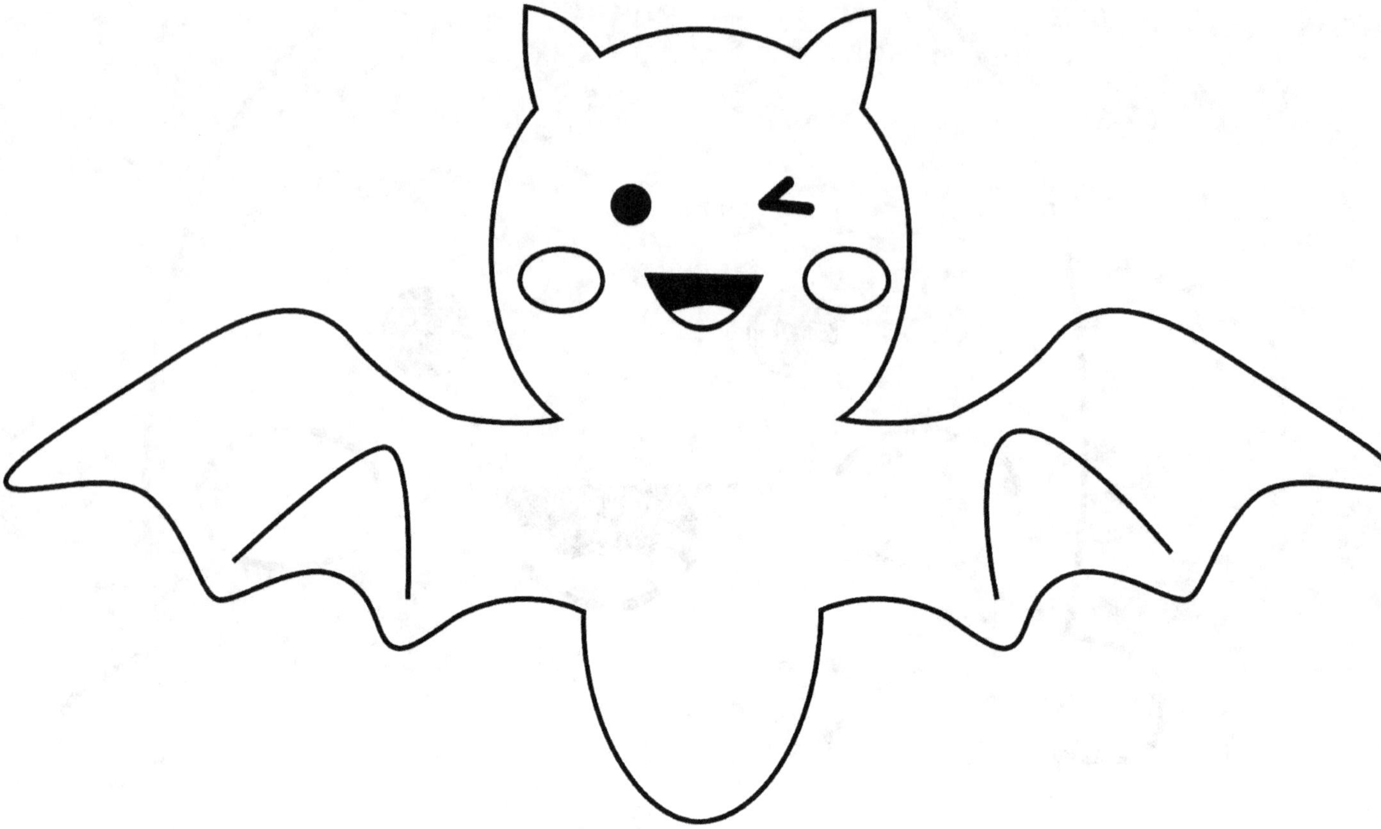

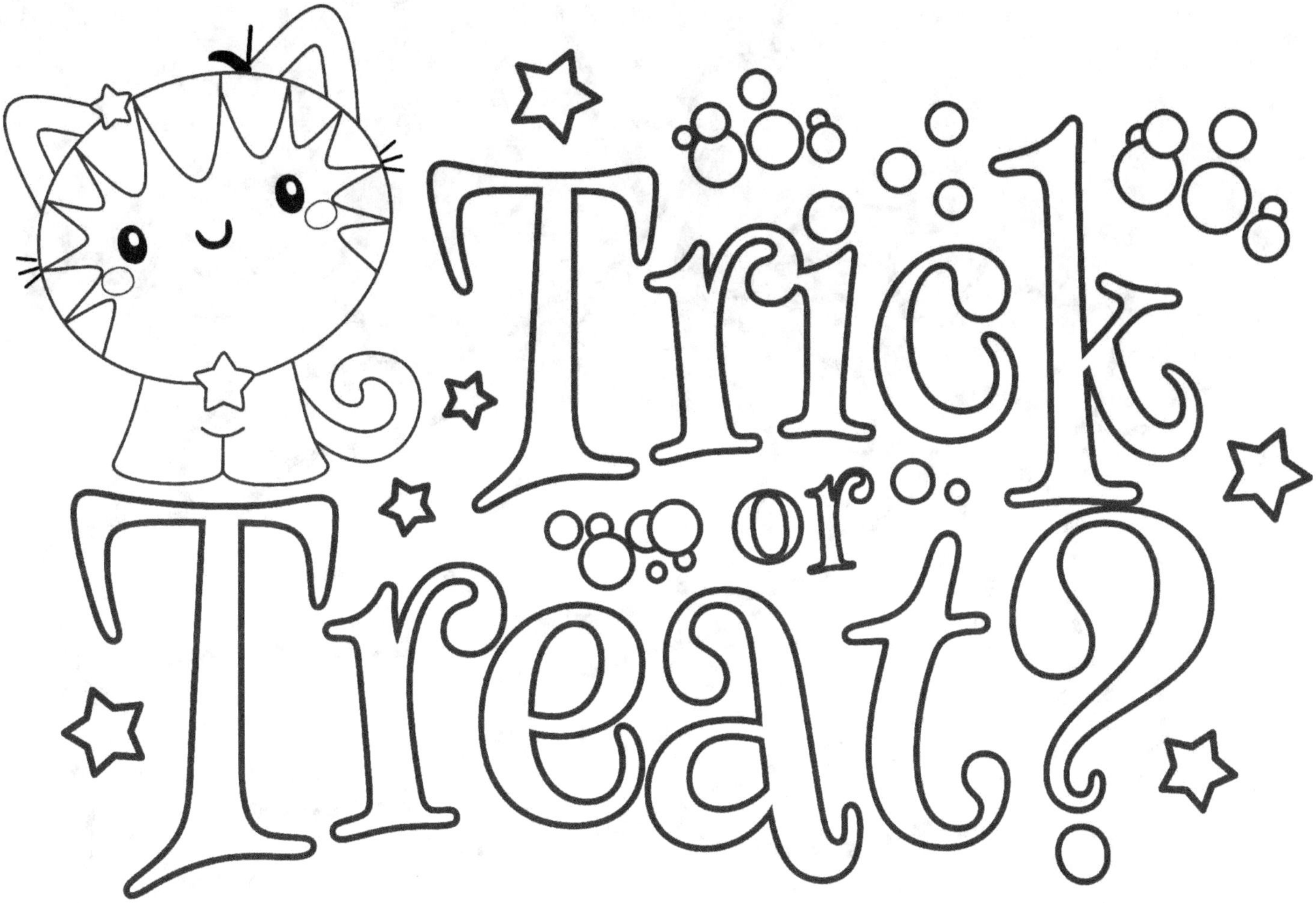
Trick
or
Treat?

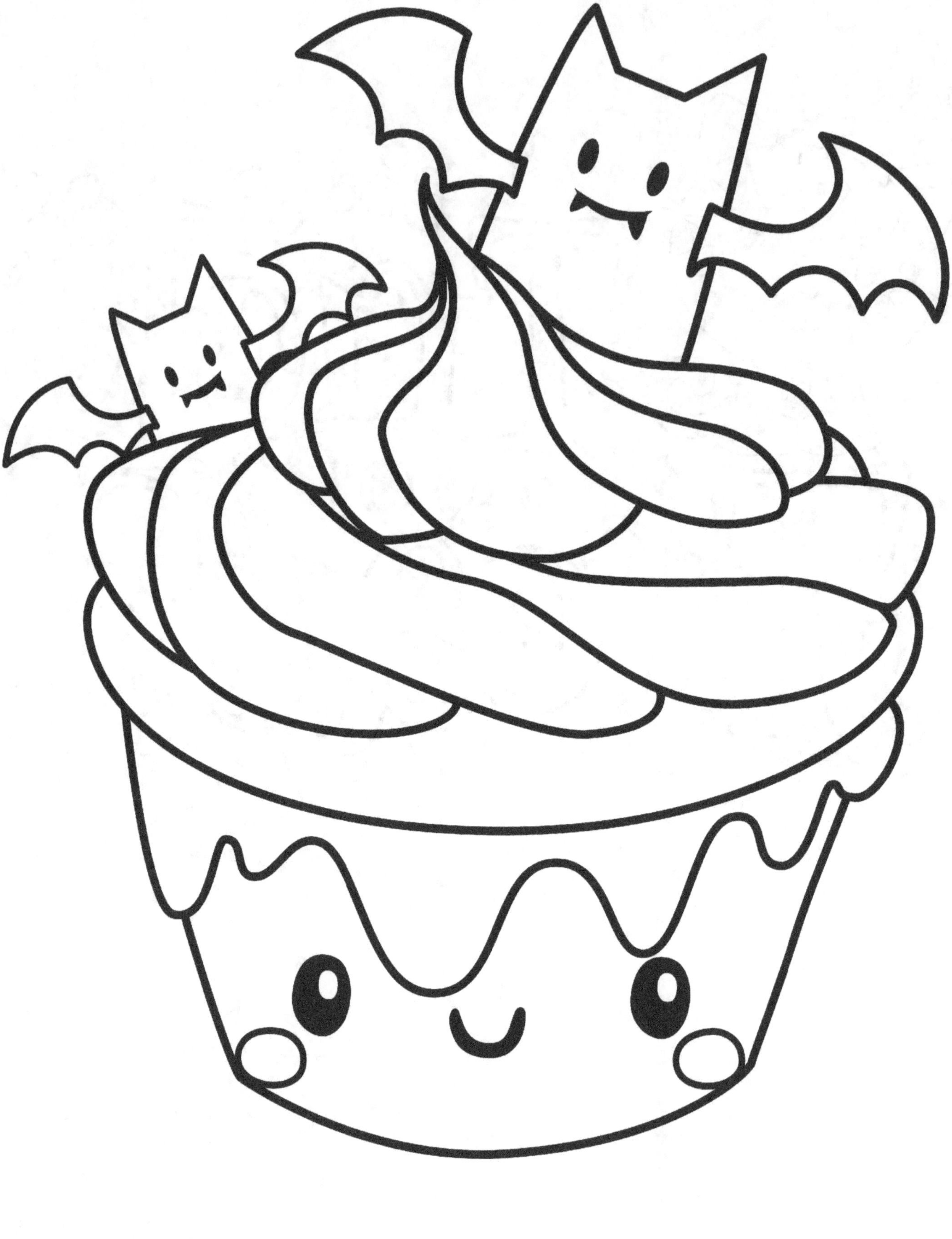

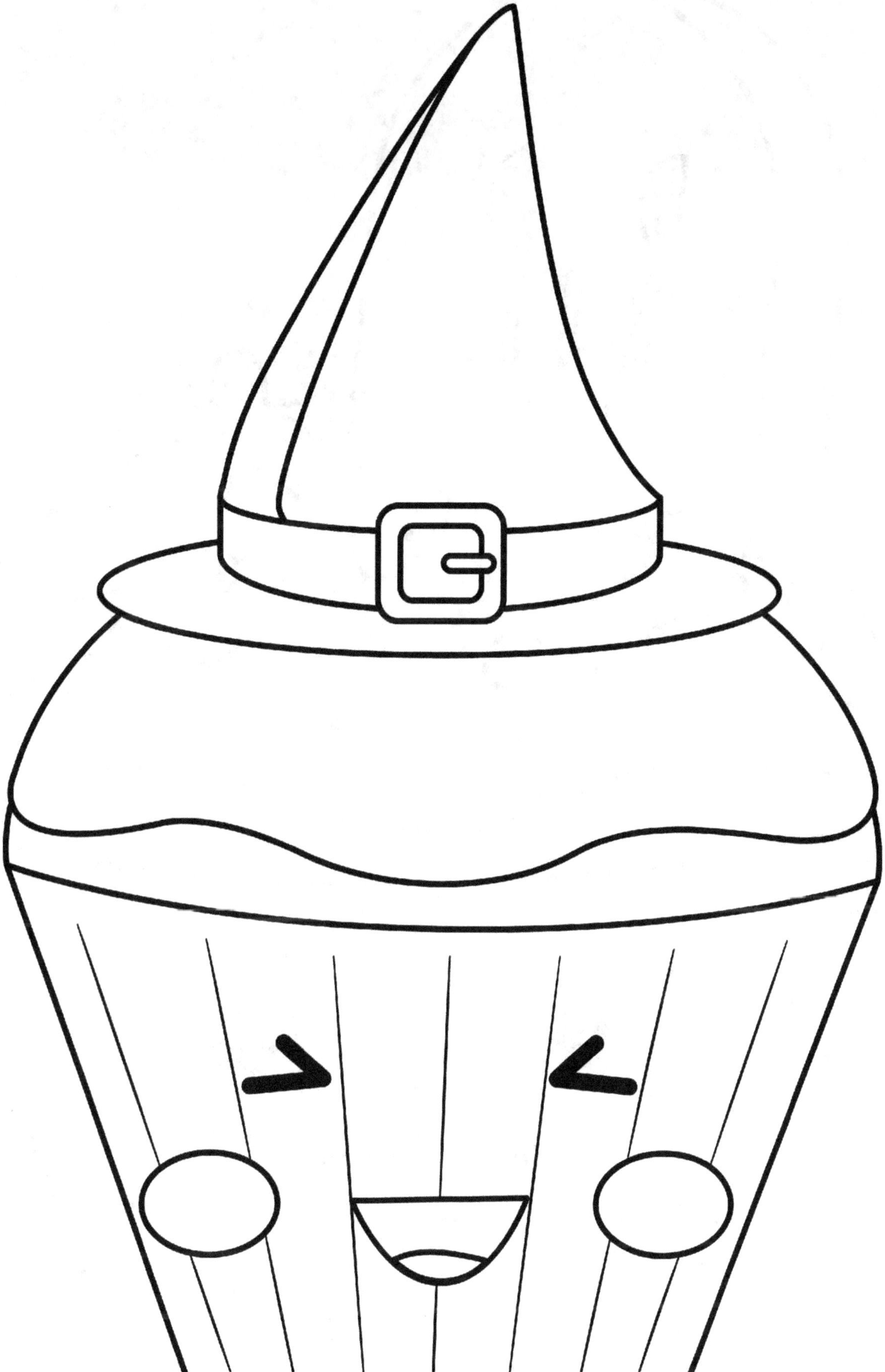

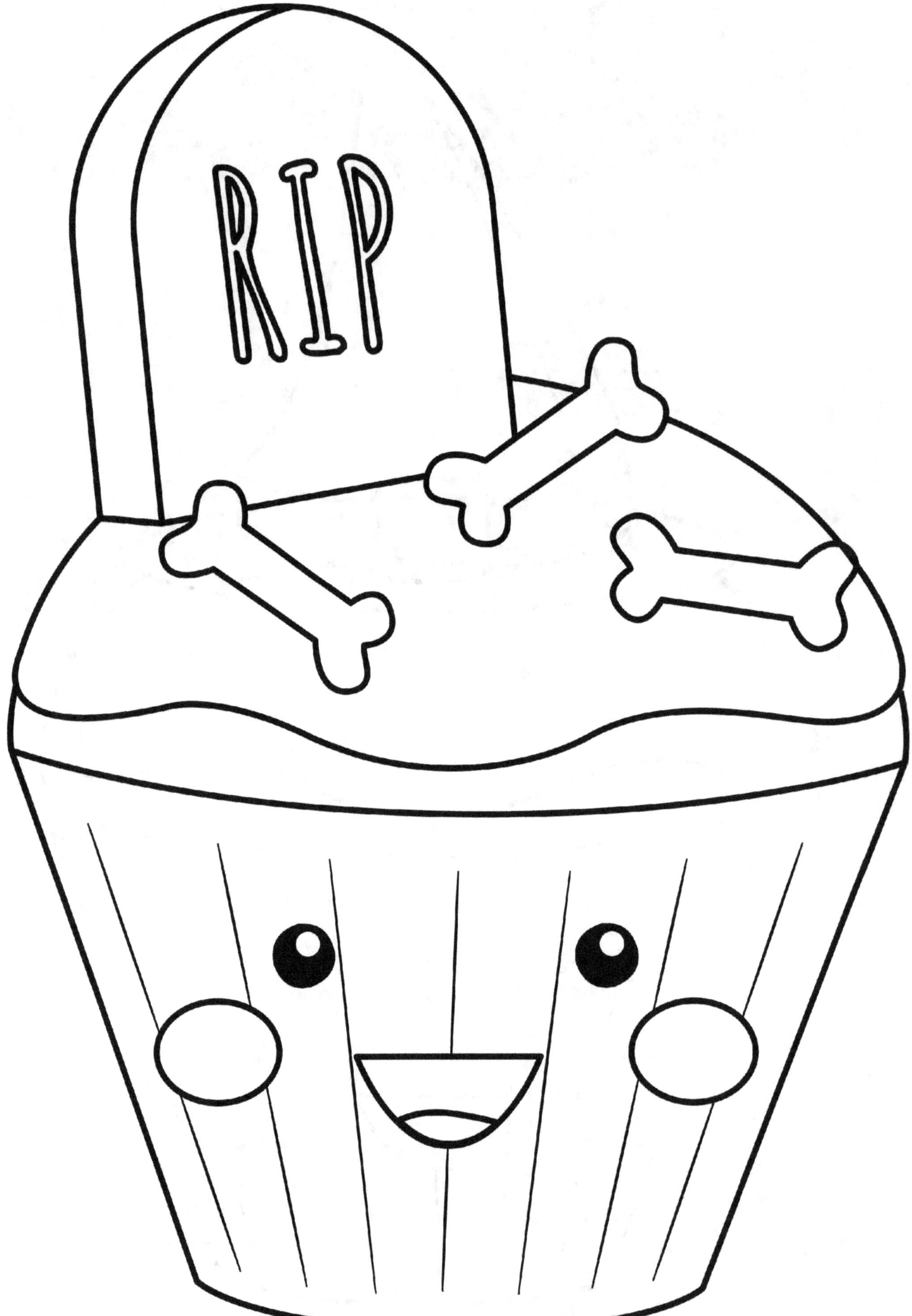
RIP

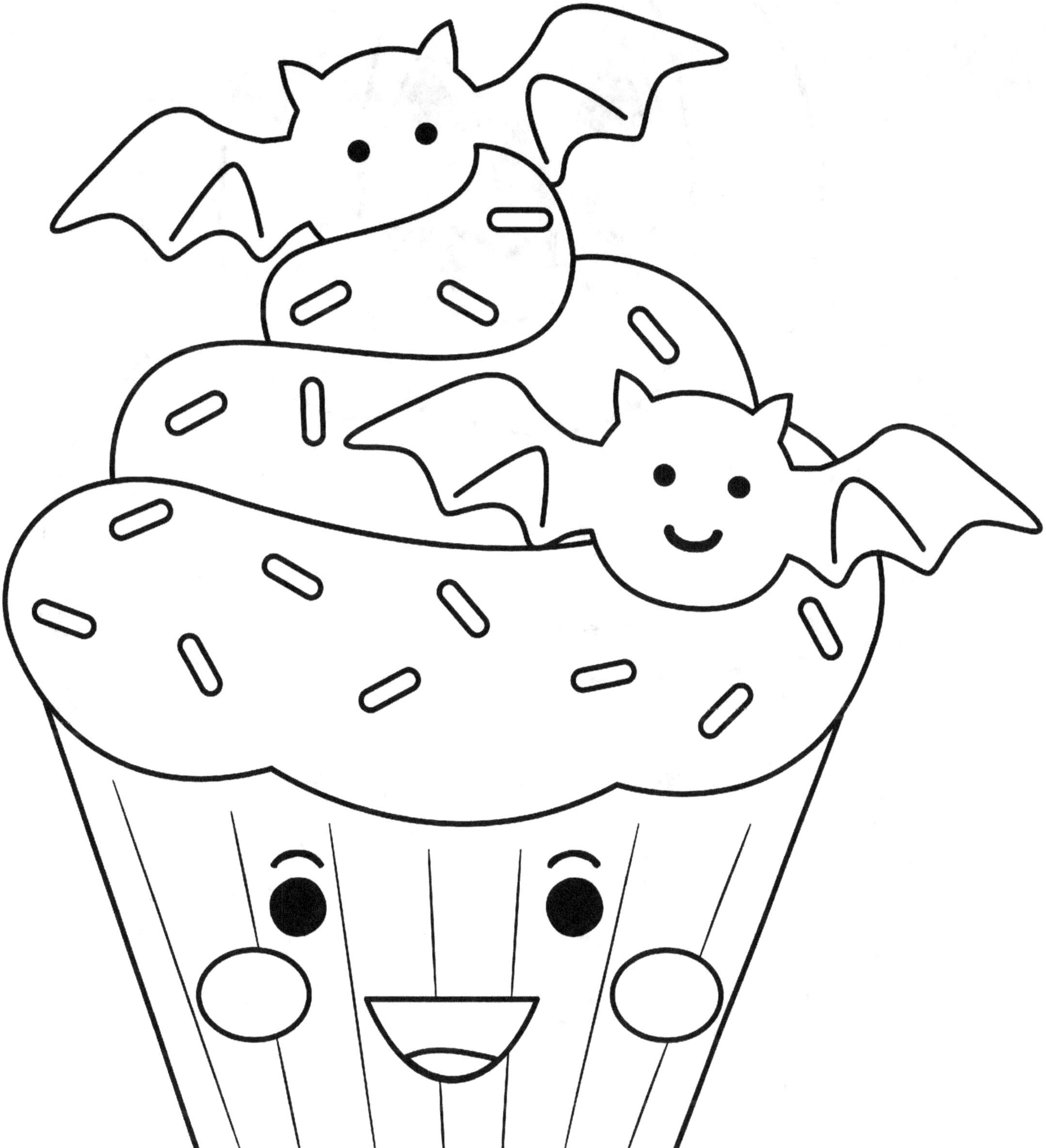

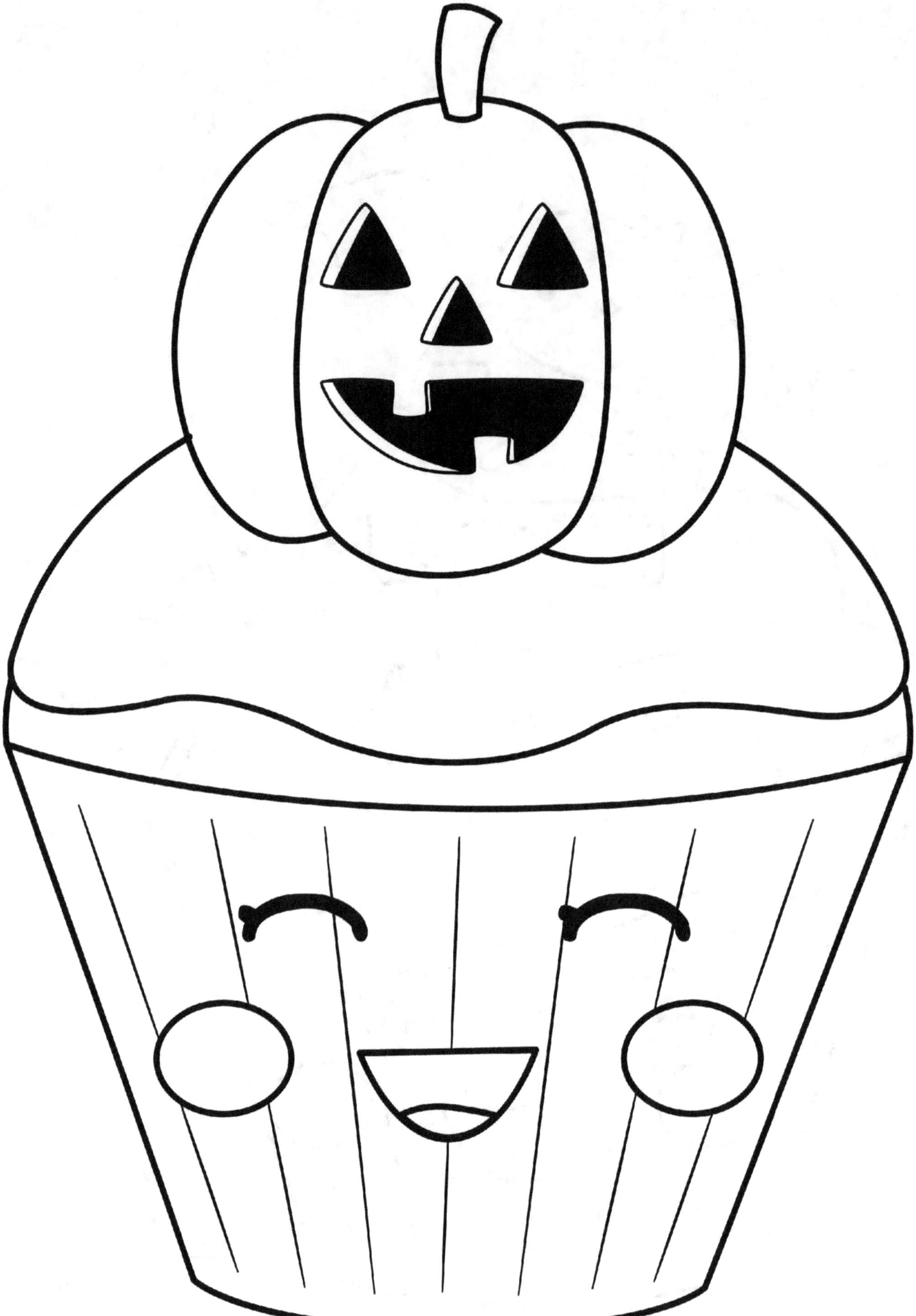

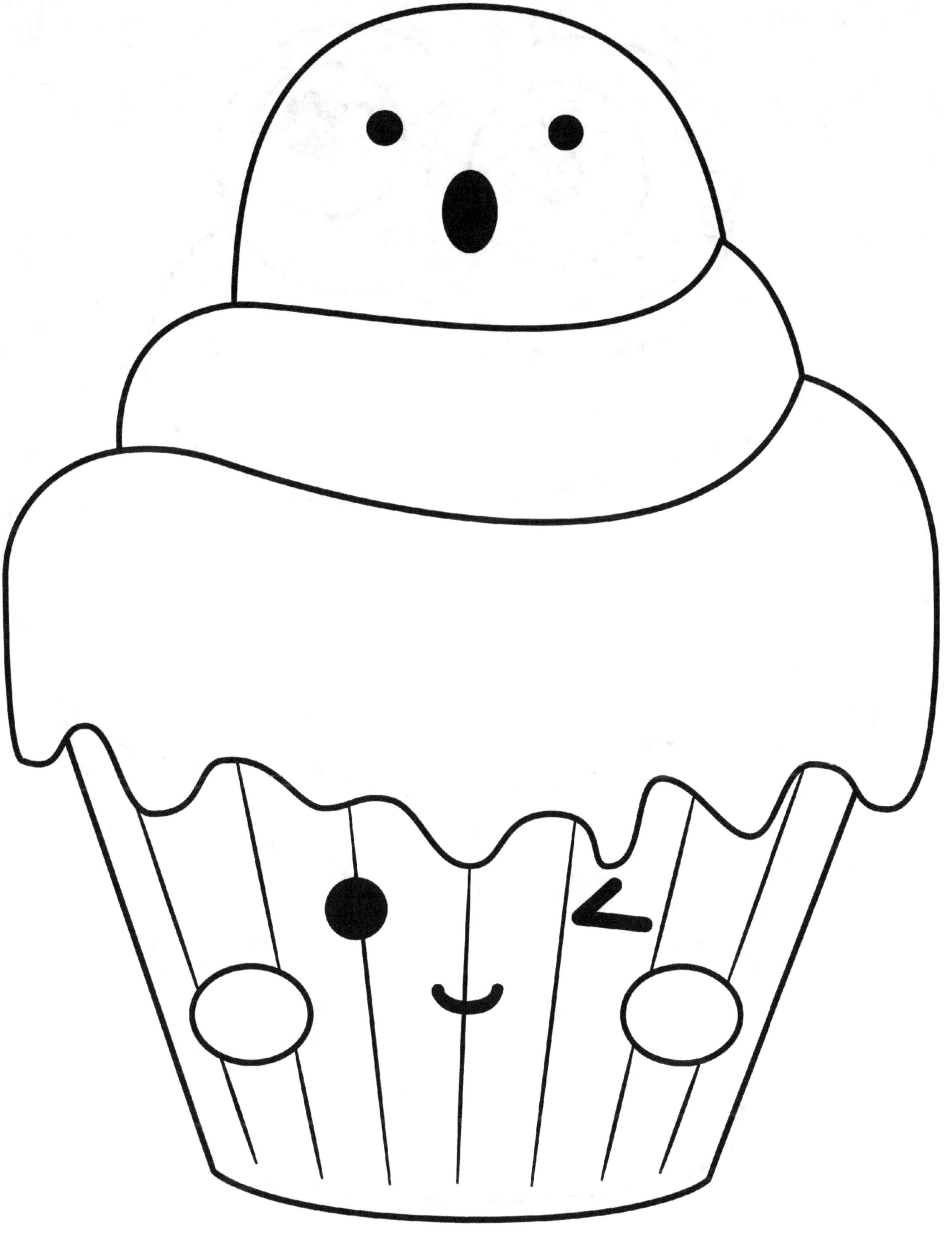

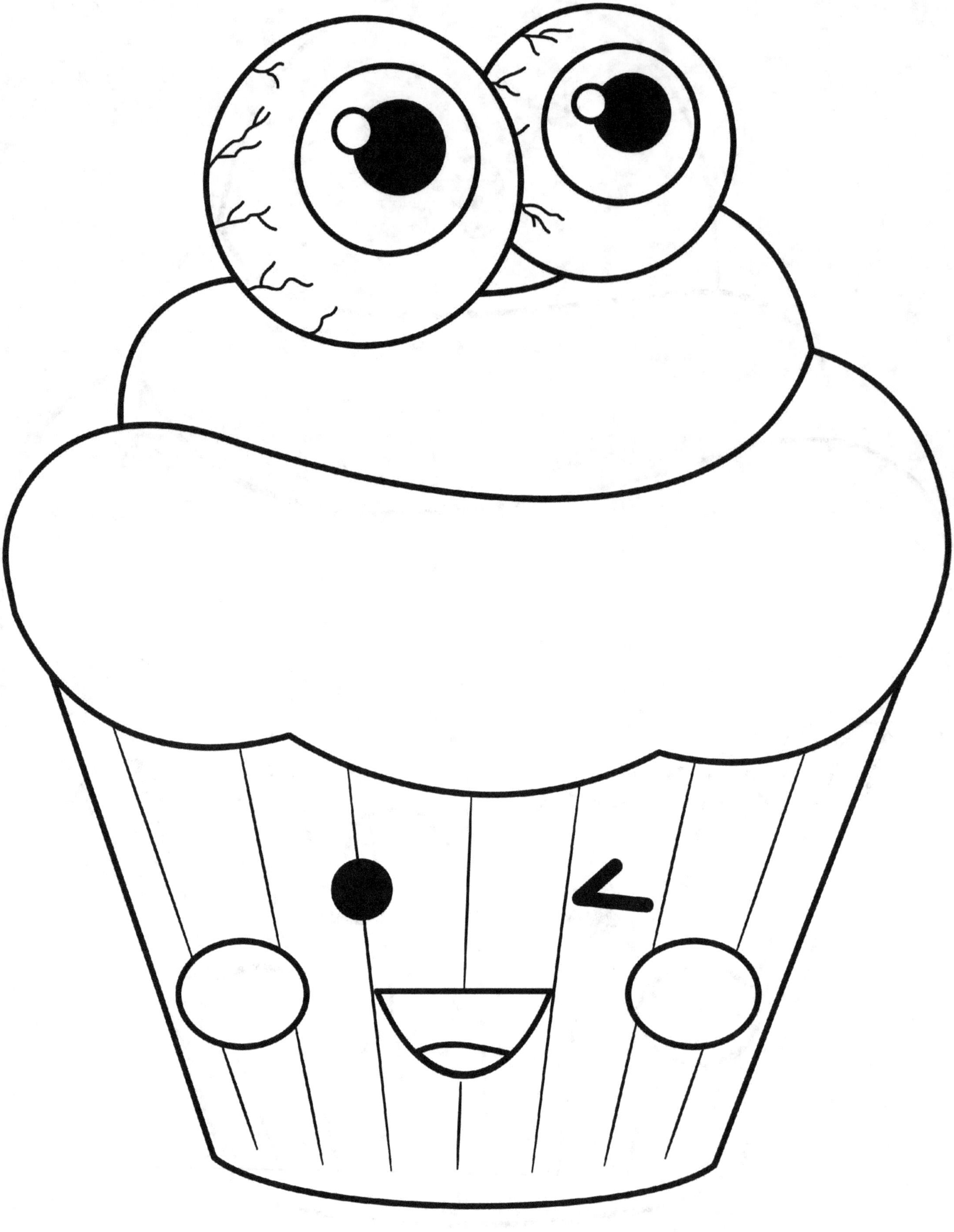

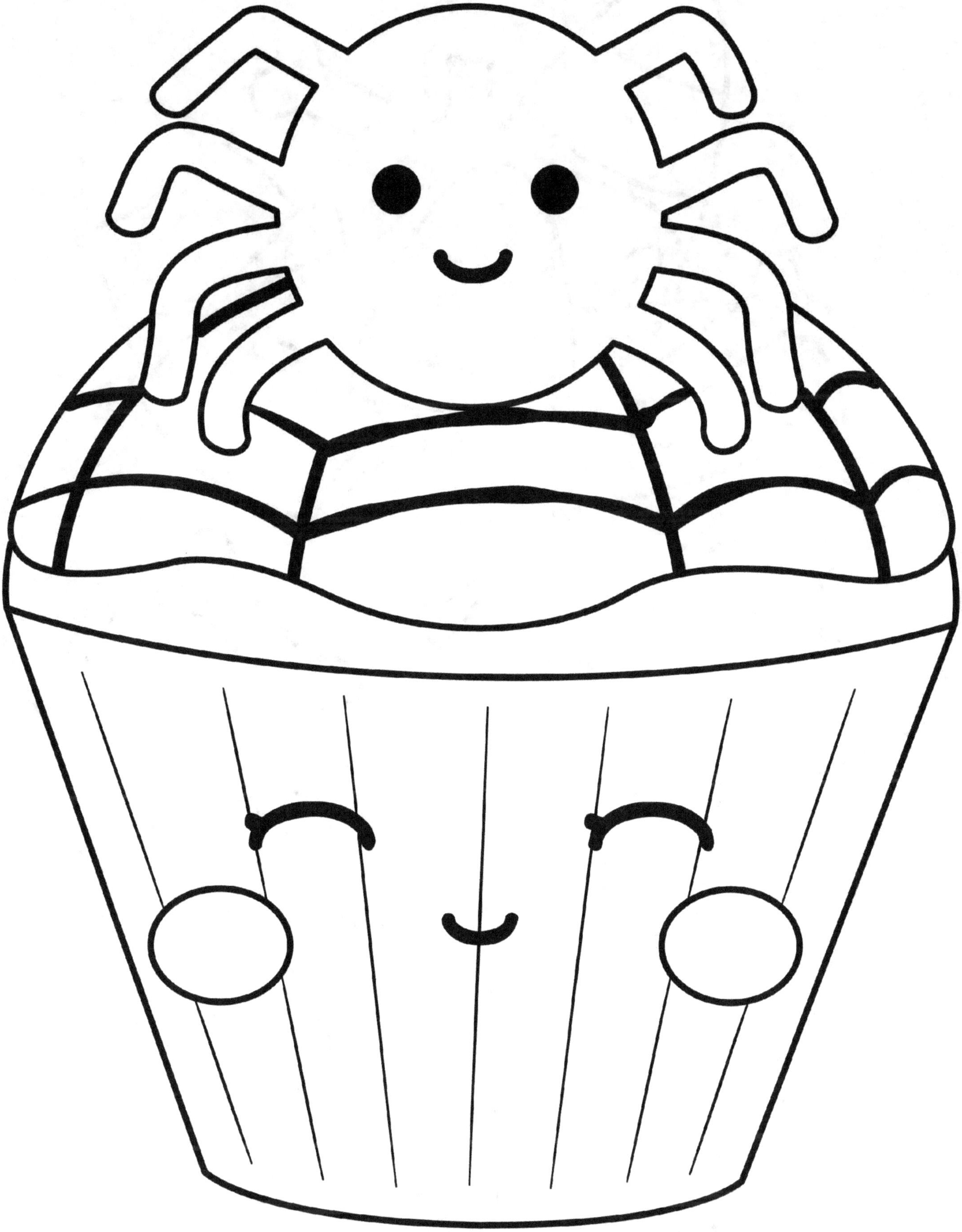

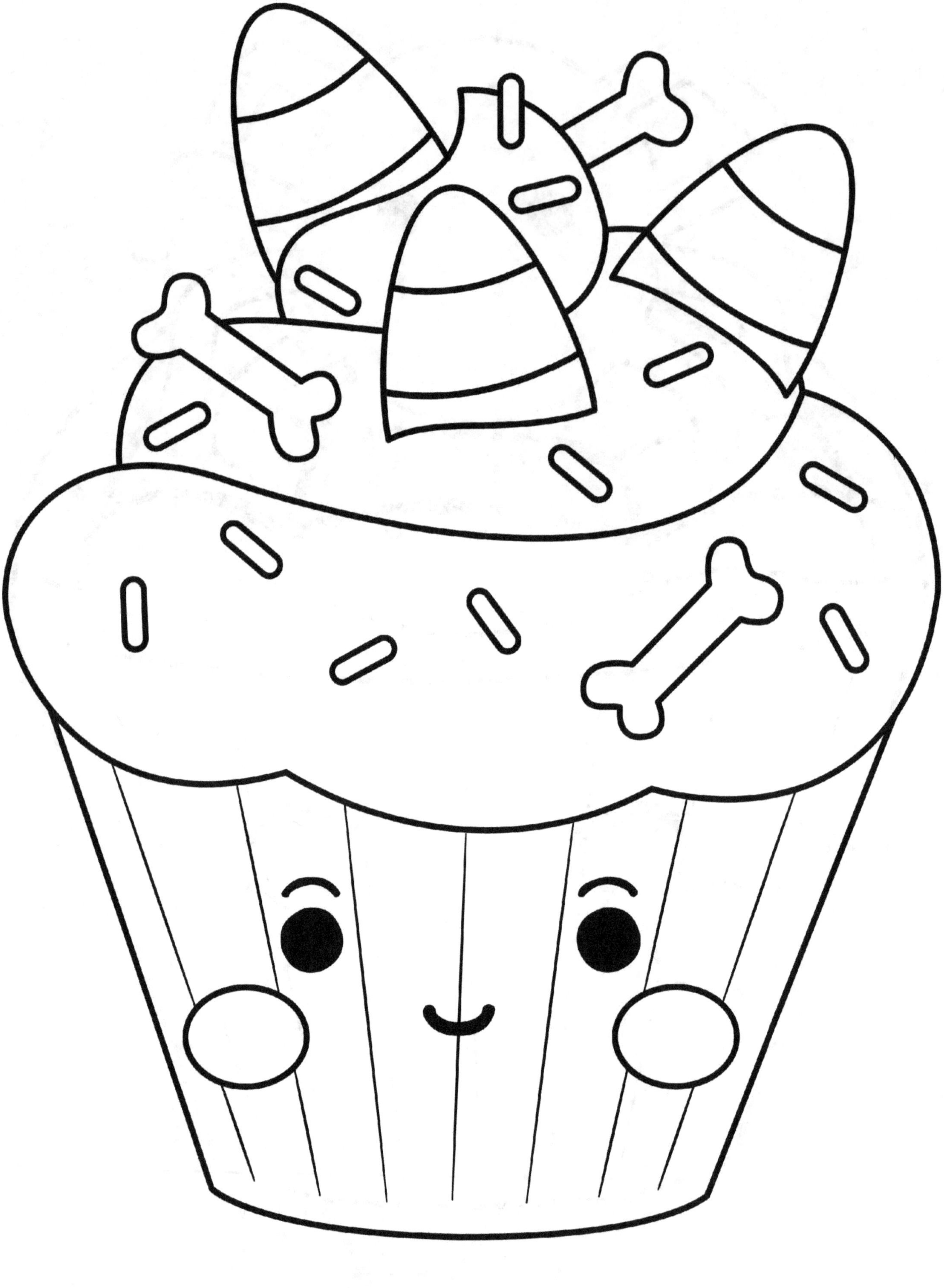

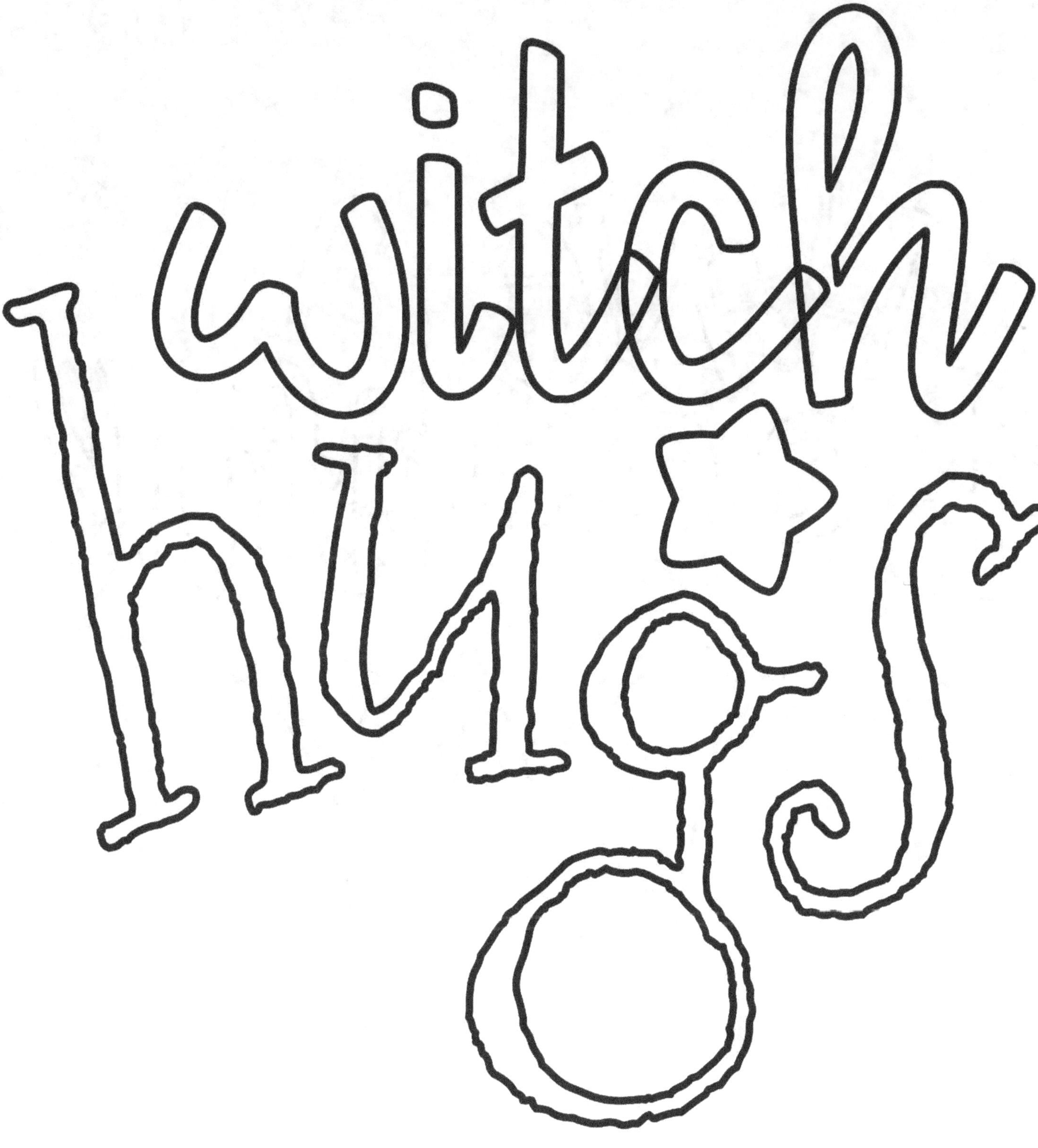
witch
hugs

Have a
Boo-tiful
DAY

www.ingramcontent.com/pod-product-compliance
Lightning Source LLC
Chambersburg PA
CBHW081703220526
45466CB00009B/2858